Vegan Bowls

First designed, printed and published June 2018 by Smudge Publishing

smudgepub.com.au

National Library of Australia

Cataloguing in Publication Data

Vegan Bowls

Includes Index

ISBN-13:978-0-646-97108-7

Smudge Culinary Travel Publishers

Vegan Bowls

A COCONUT BOWLS COOKBOOK

Contents

Welcome to Vegan Bowls: A Coconut Bowls Cookbook

We believe that eating plant-based food out of plant-based bowls is what nature intended. The recipes in this cookbook are 100 percent vegan; however, your food choices may not be. While we want to help you eat more plants, the only diet we recommend is a healthy one, whatever that looks like for you.

Positive food behaviour begins in your mind, and we want to encourage you to make healthy choices when eating out of a Coconut Bowl. Coconut Bowls are made from real coconuts, they're 100 percent natural and crafted by hand – just as your food should be.

Designed as an interactive cookbook, Vegan Bowls is one of a kind. There is no one 'author' here, in this book 100 of our favourite foodies have come together to share their favourite recipes with you. Each dish has been designed for you to recreate at home in your own Coconut Bowls.

This book is jam packed with healthy, wholesome, plant-based recipes. There are meals for breakfast, lunch and dinner, along with an abundance of tasty and easy-to-prepare snacks and raw treats to satisfy your every craving. Each recipe leaves room for your own creativity, and we encourage you to experiment, as that is exactly what our recipe developers have done. Your kitchen is a magical space where the only limit is your imagination.

Be bold, be brave and have fun.

"When I first saw Coconut Bowls, I knew that I needed them. I fell in love at first sight, but it wasn't until I first used them that I realised how much of an impact they would have on my life. I have never been a morning person, and breakfast for me has meant only a piece of toast, if anything at all. Now I go to bed excited about waking up and thinking about what I'm going to put in my morning Coconut Bowl. Introducing them to my daily life has led to becoming the healthiest I have ever been and I am more mindful about my impact on the earth. Coconut Bowls have changed my life, thank you for everything."

— Angie, Coconut Bowls customer

Community

This is a message to the wonderful Coconut Bowls community – thank you for everything. Your support and willingness to share our message has been the fundamental reason for all that we've achieved since beginning our journey in January 2016.

Seeing you enjoy such beautiful food in our Coconut Bowls puts the biggest smile on my face, and I consider myself so lucky to start each day looking at all your amazing creations.

There is a common passion shared throughout our community that I find extremely special. It is your kindness and compassion for one another and all beings and your love for preparing delicious food and gratitude towards our planet that makes me so happy.

We've created this cookbook as our way of giving thanks to those who have supported us. This book is so much more than just a cookbook; it is a collage of our community's best creative work.

In this book you will find recipes for every occasion, many of which I'm sure will become household favourites. Yet it is the stories that you'll read along the way, that I'm most excited to share with you. You'll be inspired by people from all over the world, and learn about what they do and why they do it.

Many of our contributors have overcome issues with their body image, eating disorders and other issues through their diet. If you read something that you can relate to, I encourage you to connect with these incredible people through their blogs and social media channels. It is hard not to be inspired by these people and their shared goal of supporting you and your health journey.

To our contributors – I have so much to thank you for. I consider you as role models for society, and I am grateful for all the kindness and love that you put out into the world. This book is just one example of how you regularly pay it forward, creating incredible content for the benefit of others. It is our privilege and I am honoured to be able to present your work in this book.

May this book inspire you to prepare food with love and to always eat with gratitude.

Jake McKeon
Founder of Coconut Bowls

Our Story

Have you ever asked yourself, why hasn't anyone thought of this?

While in Bali in 2015, I asked myself this exact question upon stumbling across coconut shell handicrafts at a local market. I discovered that local craftspeople were carving and painting coconut shells, and selling them to tourists as souvenirs.

I questioned whether these beautiful shells could be used to eat food from, and wondered where I could source them. The thought of what happened to coconut shells after the flesh has been taken out had never entered my mind until then.

Through research, I discovered that billions of these shells were going to waste every year. As a bi-product of the thriving coconut industry, coconut shells have traditionally been burned or discarded as landfill. I thought it was interesting that these shells – shaped almost perfectly to be used as a bowl – were considered waste.

A local craftsman taught me that coconut shells have been used as bowls in his, and many other villages for hundreds of years. I had never seen this at home in Australia and thought that maybe people would like them.

I asked my new friend if he could make some for me and then packed as many as I could into my luggage and returned to Australia. The thought of quarantine and customs hadn't entered my mind until I was stopped with a surfboard cover and suitcase full of

these weird, yet wonderful looking bowls. Fortunately, because the husk had been sanded off and they were sealed (originally with beeswax, now with organic coconut oil made from their flesh), they passed through without issue. After a couple of posts on Instagram, people from all over the world began asking if they could buy them.

After selling our first bowl in January 2016, we now reclaim over 10,000 discarded coconut shells every month. We purchase them from coconut farmers who had previously spent precious money and resources on the waste process. We take the coconut shells to one of our ethical workshops in Vietnam and Indonesia, where we employ local craftspeople at well above fair trade standards. Our team cuts, sands and polishes these coconut shells into beautiful coconut bowls that are food safe, reusable and can last a lifetime. We think they're the perfect eco-friendly addition to any kitchen.

Every coconut bowl is unique, with its own shape, size, marking and imperfections. They're one in a billion, just like you. This means that nobody else in the world will have a coconut bowl just like yours. Now that is pretty cool, isn't it?

Jake McKeon
Founder of Coconut Bowls

Learn more about Coconut Bowls at
coconutbowls.com
@coconutbowls

Plant-Based Eating

Plant-based eating and Coconut Bowls go hand in hand. There's something special about eating from a natural bowl filled with only food that can be grown and picked from your garden.

Whether you follow a vegetarian or vegan diet or are simply trying to eat more plants and fewer animal products, this book will show you just how delicious plant-based food is. Many of the recipes have been inspired by traditional meals that you will have grown up with. These dishes have been developed through creativity and thinking outside the box and as you'll soon experience, taste as good as or even better than the original.

When we eat more food from plant sources, our intake of vital nutrients including fibre, antioxidants, vitamins and minerals increase. Boosting our nutrient intake positively impacts the way we feel, and when we consume more whole, plant-based foods we tend to see an increase in energy, clearer skin and find it easier to lose weight.

While a strictly plant-based diet may not be for everyone, if we all include more plant-based meals in our diet, we will all be better off. This book has been created to showcase how incredibly tasty and versatile plant-based foods are, and to inspire you to embrace a more sustainable and healthy lifestyle with ease.

Sustainability

Sustainability can be defined as 'meeting the needs of the present without compromising the ability of future generations to meet theirs'.

Environmental sustainability involves participating every day in making positive decisions that will foster a sustainable future for humans and all beings alike.

Reduce, Reuse, Recycle: this mantra has been around for decades, but there's never been a more important time to embrace it than today. Reducing our waste is the most vital choice here, and it is the easiest for us to do.

Every year trillions of 'one-use' plastics and disposable objects end up as landfill. From takeaway coffee cups to packaging waste and plastic straws, it is hard to ignore the endless amount of waste products that we are disposing of on a daily basis. While we would all love for product manufacturers to change their ways, it is up to us first as consumers to change our behaviour.

By making small changes, we can make a huge difference across our lifetime. A simple example of a way that we can all participate is by giving up disposable coffee cups and bringing your own reusable cup. For a coffee-a-day drinker, you could save over 365 cups every year, and if you can encourage 10 friends to join you, that is over 3650 each year!

Encouraging businesses to change begins with us as consumers no longer accepting unsustainable practices. Just like Coconut Bowls, there are many eco-friendly options made from plants, like biodegradable bamboo products and plates made from palm leaves.

Together we can make a significant impact. The reason sustainability is so important is very simple: our future and the future of our children depend on it.

Nutrition Basics

Sustainable, healthy, plant-based eating is easy – if you have the right nutritional know-how. The basics include eating a variety of foods, such as colourful fruits and vegetables (and lots of nutritious leafy greens), as well as wholesome wholegrains, healthy proteins and plant-based milks.

Australian dietitian, Jacinta Sultana, believes a healthy diet is one that includes fruit, vegetables and grains. A combination of these ingredients form the basis of many of our recipes – and for all the right reasons.

Macronutrients and micronutrients, we have heard of them but what do they actually mean? To make smart food choices that satisfy our nutritional needs, it is important that we understand both.

MACRONUTRIENTS

These are required in large volumes to provide energy with carbohydrates, proteins and fats the three primary sources. Each of these macronutrients is important. Carbohydrates are broken down into glucose, our primary energy source. Protein is broken down into amino acids, necessary for building and repairing muscle tissue. Fats, likewise, are an essential part of a healthy diet improving energy, vitamin absorption, cellular structure and much more!

MICRONUTRIENTS

These are not required in the same volumes as macronutrients, but that does not make them any less important! Vitamins and minerals are the rockstars here, contributing significantly to both our physical and mental wellbeing. Without proper consumption of vitamins and minerals we become much more susceptible to a host of illnesses and diseases. The best part about micronutrients? Your favourite fruits and vegetables are loaded with them! We will eat to that.

Jacinta Sultana
Dietitian, Sunshine Coast

Vegetables contain a laundry list of essential micronutrients, and are often high in fibre and low in calories – go ahead, fill your bowls up! They are a good source of carbohydrate and often protein. In our eyes there's no such thing as a bad vegetable.

— JACINTA SULTANA

Veggies

Cooking recommendations for optimum taste and nutrition

Cooking changes the colour, texture, taste and nutritional content of vegetables.

- Colour: Heat breaks down enzymes and stabilises proteins, making green colours more vibrant.
- Nutrients: Water leaches out water-soluble vitamins like vitamins B and C, and water-soluble phytonutrients like the purple colour in purple cabbage, or beetroot. Adding oil to a stir-fry, or dressing, makes fat-soluble vitamins, such as beta-carotene in carrots (which our body converts to vitamin A).
- Texture: The combination of heat and time makes vegetables softer and easier to eat and digest.
- Flavour: Flavours change, as some components of fresh, 'green' flavour are lost due to heat, sugars can caramelise (go brown) producing new flavours, or bitter flavours can become more dominant.

Steaming (for a maximum of three minutes) leaves vegetables brightly coloured, crunchy and tasting great, and minimises loss of water-soluble vitamins like vitamin C.

Stir-frying (for a maximum of three minutes) allows vegetables to retain their hue, crunch and taste. The addition of oil makes fat-soluble vitamins and phytonutrients more available to your body.

Oven-baking is great for root and starchy vegetables such as potatoes, making the energy and fibre available, and caramelising the sugars to make them taste great. Although the heat reduces some vitamins, the lack of water maintains others.

Nutritional information sourced from Veggycation by Horticulture Innovation Australia and Sunshine Coast-based dietitian, Jacinta Sultana

POTATO

Starchy vegetables, such as the humble potato, have a valuable place on the plate of anyone looking to power up their meal. They contain a range nutrients, and can be enjoyed all year round. Your cooking options are endless, but we particularly like them roasted and served crunchy.

BEETROOT

Beetroot is rich in vitamins and minerals. They can be eaten raw, a nice addition to your favourite salad, but are even more popular cooked! Cooking creates a sweetness so perfect you'll find excuses to cook them more often. Beetroot is at its finest in spring, summer and autumn (fall) purchased fresh from your local greengrocer.

CAULIFLOWER

Cauliflower has grown in popularity the past few years, which we absolutely love. Cauliflower rice, mash, tortillas, hummus, crust... the list goes on! While many people eat only the florets, the stem and leaves are edible and great for soups and stocks. Make use of this versatile vegetable all year round.

ONION

Onions have been a part of the human diet for more than 7000 years, and for good reason. They are often cooked, adding flavour and sweetness to savoury dishes that we all love. Cutting onions makes you cry? We hear you! Try cutting them under a slow stream of running water. Onions are available all year round.

CARROT

Carrots, delicious carrots. Popular raw, sliced thin onto a salad or whole with a favourite spread, r roasted and stir-fried to caramelise its natural sugars. They are in season throughout summer, autumn (fall) and winter. And while many of us associate carrots with the colour orange, they can also be red, white, yellow and purple.

PUMPKIN

Forget Halloween, we are enjoying pumkin all year round! Unlike other vegetables which can be eaten raw, the benefit of pumpkin is released when cooked, giving your body unrestricted access its nutrients. Cut thick slices of pumpkin before spicing, roasting and serving with a tantalising green salad.

Fruit, magical fruit. Fruit is full of essential vitamins and minerals, is great for energy and contains water to help keep you hydrated. Fibre is the superhero though, which is essential for optimum gut health and overall wellbeing.

— JACINTA SULTANA

Fruit

Fruit sugar

Natural sugar is the major source of carbohydrate in fruit, the majority of which is 'fructose' – a simple carbohydrate. Although fructose has been given a bad name by the 'no-sugar' movement, these naturally occurring fruit sugars can still be part of a healthy diet. Fruit contains a multitude of beneficial nutrients as well as a little bit of natural sugar, unlike processed and sugar-sweetened drinks or foods, which tend to contain too much sugar and too little nutrients. Balance and moderation is the key.

Two kinds of fibre

When we think of food fibre, we tend to think of roughage – the crunchy, stringy coarse kind of fibre. This is also known as insoluble fibre. It is good for gut health and helps food transit through the intestines. However, the oft-forgotten soluble fibre, which absorbs water and becomes gel-like during digestion, can help alleviate constipation. Both kinds of fibre exist in different ratios in food such as fruit, vegetables, legumes and whole grains.

BERRIES

Blueberries, blackberries, strawberries, raspberries and acai berries. Bright, sweet and flavourful superfuits with a long list of benefits. We love their antioxidant power, empowering the body to fight inflammation. Berries are also high in fibre and lower in sugar - more reasons to feel good reaching for that second handful.

BANANAS

When nature packages a fruit so perfectly, we pay attention. Native to Southeast Asia, bananas are now grown in many warmer parts of the world and are among the most popular fruits on earth. Perfect for peeling and eating on the go, they are also the perfect addition to morning yogurt (coconut for us, please!), overnight oats or creamy smoothie bowls.

ORANGES

A soft, juicy and pulpy citrus fruit, oranges are known for delivering a delicious dose of Vitamin C, important for warding of any seasonal colds your colleagues might be carrying. Valencia oranges are in season spring to autumn (fall), and navels are in season late autumn (fall) to early summer.

MANGO

Our quintessential summer fruit, no food reminds us of sun, sand and surf quite like a ripe Mango. We suggest trying them fresh, frozen and grilled to enjoy their sweetness - take your pick! They are a summer fruit and are usually available throughout summer and autumn (fall).

PINEAPPLE

It takes nearly 3 years for a pineapple to mature, but only seconds to appreciate its unique appearance and flavour. Once picked, pineapple will not continue to ripen so there is no need to wait, simply cut and enjoy this tropical fruit at the first available opportunity.

PASSIONFRUIT

We are drawn to Kiwifruit for its exotic taste and radiant green flesh, but do not discard the skin. It delivers a punch of nutrition with plenty of fiber to keep digestion regular. Simply remove the hard ends and voilà. They are available year round, but reach their peak in autumn (fall) and winter.

KIWIFRUIT

We are drawn to Kiwifruit for its exotic taste and radiant green flesh, but do not discard the skin. It delivers a punch of nutrition with plenty of fiber to keep digestion regular. Simply remove the hard ends and voilà. They are available year round, but reach their peak in autumn (fall) and winter.

PAPAYA

Papaya, pawpaw and papaw. Confused? So were we! Until discovering they refer to the same fruit. We are particularly fond of papain, an enzyme found in papaya that aids digestion. Once exotic and rare, papaya is now available year round with greater supplies spring and autumn (fall).

AVOCADO

Avocados are universally loved for their rich, creamy texture and taste.
Equally nutritious as they are delicious, it is their healthy, mono-unsaturated fats that we are fond of, which makes avocado a great food to include in your diet sliced, smashed or in a smoothie.

WATERMELON

Containing around 90 per cent moisture, the name 'watermelon' is fitting. However, lets not dismiss watermelon as a simple combination of water and sugar. It contains a high amount of lycopene, an antioxidant said to both protect and repair the body. Watermelons are readily available throughout spring and summer.

APPLES & PEARS

Rich sources of soluble fibre, apples and pears are best eaten with their skin on. Both fruits lend themselves perfectly to 'grab and go', but we also love slicing and serving them with a big salad. Crisp pear, fresh arugula, roasted walnuts, ripe avocado and a balsamic vinaigrette, yum!

TOMATOES

Tomatoes are around 94 percent water and low in sugar (only 2.4 grams of carbohydrates per 100 grams). Perfect for sauces, salsas, soups and sandwiches, how do you prefer yours? Abundant in summer and autumn (fall), they are also available tinned and preserved all year round.

Leafy greens – such as kale, spinach, bok choy and broccoli – are high in protein and contain common nutrients that can be troublesome for those of us following a plant-based diet to get adequate supplies of, such as calcium and iron.

— JACINTA SULTANA

Greens

The benefit of greens

We have always been told to eat our greens, but why? Green vegetables are rich in phytonutrients, including flavonoids and carotenoids, which are associated with reduced risk of a variety of diseases. Not only will they keep you healthy, they also ensure you feel amazing each and every day. With so many amazing greens to choose from, remember variety is the spice of life! Each vegetable offers its own unique taste and nutrition - we encourage you to include a number of different greens in your diet.

Raw versus cooked

While a number of vegetables can be enjoyed cooked, Jacinta is an advocate of enjoying them raw when possible. When vegetables are cooked some damage is done to the nutrients in them. It is great to include raw vegetables a couple of times per day in your diet.

How to use

Greens are the perfect sidekick or base to any bowl. Whether you choose to eat fresh, or lightly cook, there is no replacement for consuming a variety of greens in your daily diet.

ALFALFA SPROUTS

Alfalfa sprouts are popular in salads and sandwiches for their fresh taste. They're actually a form of legume in sprouted form, and contain some folate and vitamin C. You can buy sprout-growing kits to grow your own sprouts at home, or they can be found in some supermarkets all year round.

BROCCOLI

Broccoli is a good source of vitamin K and vitamin C and also contains plenty of fibre, potassium and folate. Broccoli is often cooked, but it is also delicious raw. The stalk and stem can be used to add crunch and texture to salads, or cooked into soups or stocks. It is available all year round.

BRUSSEL SPROUTS

These mini cabbage lookalikes are actually edible buds. They are a member of the brassica family and are a good source of vitamins, as well as fibre and potassium. Brussels sprouts can be eaten raw, stir-fried or roasted. They are in season in spring and winter.

CABBAGE

Cabbage is rich in fibre, potassium and folate. It can be eaten raw, say in a colorful slaw, but it shines brightest when pickled, stir-fried or roasted. Fresh cabbage is available spring, summer and autumn (fall).

ZUCCHINI

Zucchini is a versatile vegetable that can be consumed both raw and cooked with a tasty yet subtle flavour. As a low calorie veggie, it can be substituted for pasta for a great base and texture to any salad.

ASIAN GREENS

Leafy Asian greens like bok choy and choy sum are an excellent source of A, B, C, E and K vitamins, and are easy ingredients to include in your diet. Available all year round, these veggies add great flavour and texture to meals and can cooked or used in a variety of ways.

ROCKET

Rocket (also called arugula) is a great source of vitamins K and A, and a 50-gram serve contains 10 percent of your recommended daily intake of calcium. It has a spicy, peppery flavour and is best consumed fresh to preserve nutrients, but can be stirred into risottos or warm salads. Rocket is available all year round.

SPINACH

Mild and versatile - salad base, smoothie add-in and superfood side - spinach is a staple in many kitchens. It is a discrete way to charge up your health without the peppery punch of arugula or pronounced flavour of kale. Fresh spinach is available in winter, spring and autumn (fall), but can be purchased frozen all year round. Green smoothies, anyone?

KALE

Kale, a source of essential vitamins and minerals, has been hailed a superfood for all the right reasons and offers more versatility than meets the eye. We will always enjoy it as a salad, dressed with fresh lemon and a quality olive oil, but we now look to this green for nutritious soups, smoothies and pesto.

LETTUCE

Head lettuces, such as iceberg, are the most popular, but there are other loose-leaf lettuces such as endive and salad greens. Lettuce has a high water content and contains some vitamin B3, helping the body to produce energy. Most lettuces are available all year round.

SILVERBEET

Silverbeet, also known as Swiss chard, can have a white or coloured stalk, with the latter often sold as rainbow chard. Silverbeet is terrific raw, but can be stir fried or steamed. It is in season throughout spring and winter.

WATERCRESS

Watercress has a peppery flavour that makes it a great addition to sandwiches and salads. It is a member of the brassica family, and is a useful source of folate for the development of red and white blood cells. Watercress is generally available all year round.

Grains are important in a balanced healthy diet, unless you have allergies or intolerances, of course. They provide great carbohydrate, protein, fibre and – in terms of minerals – are important for zinc, B vitamins, iron, selenium, phosphorus and magnesium.

— JACINTA SULTANA

Grains

What is a whole grain?

A whole grain is a cereal grain that still contains its bran, endosperm and germ. The bran is the outer skin of a grain that is high in fibre and contains vitamins, minerals and fibre. The endosperm contains proteins and carbohydrates, and the germ is rich in fatty acids, vitamin E, B vitamins and other plant nutrients.

Whole grains contain a number of nutrients that are not found in processed grains, or grains that have had the bran and germ removed – such as white rice. Nutrients and phytonutrients which are plant nutrients that are thought to play a role in maintaining overall health.

Being gluten free

Grains such as wheat, rye, barley and oats contain a protein called gluten – it is what gives bread its chewy texture and helps bind flour-based products together. However, for those with coeliac disease or gluten intolerance, it can cause bowel damage and digestive discomfort respectively. The good news is, a number of healthy whole grains are gluten free.

Nutritional information sourced from the Grains and Legumes Nutrition Council glnc.org.au

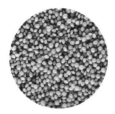

AMARANTH

Amaranth is a small, round pseudo-cereal – meaning it is actually a seed. It is high in protein and contains lysine – an amino acid that is not present in many other grains. Amaranth also contains some iron, magnesium, potassium and appreciable amounts of calcium. It has a fresh, peppery taste that makes it great for savoury dishes, and is gluten free.

How to cook amaranth
Amaranth can be boiled for around 20 minutes to create a gluten-free porridge, and puffed amaranth is becoming popular as a gluten-free cereal alternative. It can also be cooked with rice (using around one part grains to two parts water) for a higher protein side dish.

BARLEY

A large portion of the world's barley crop is used to make beer. However, it is also great for adding texture to soups and salads. Barley is low in fat and high in carbohydrates and contains a number of B vitamins, as well as some iron, magnesium and calcium. Barley is also a source of beta-glucan, a type of fibre that may lower cholesterol.

How to cook barley
Pearl barley (made by removing the coarse outer layers of the grain) and scotch barley (de-husked and roughly ground grain) are often boiled into soups and stews. Otherwise, barley can be cooked similar to rice; simply cover the grain with water and boil until tender. Barley keeps its texture even when cooked extensively.

BUCKWHEAT

Buckwheat is a pseudo-cereal. It is technically not a grain, but actually a seed that is closely related to the rhubarb plant. It is high in protein and carbohydrates and rich in polyunsaturated fatty acids. Buckwheat also contains resistant starch, which can help support good gut health. Plus, it is gluten free.

How to cook buckwheat
Buckwheat groats can be soaked overnight and then dried/dehydrated and eaten raw. But they're also popular toasted (often called kasha) and added to salads or stirred into porridge for added crunch. Buckwheat flour is also popular, and can be used to make gluten-free pancakes, noodles and other products.

FARRO

Farro (also known as emmer) is a kind of whole grain wheat that is high in antioxidants, fibre and carbohydrates, but low in fat. It is also a source of B vitamins, potassium, magnesium and vitamin E. It has a nutty taste and chewy texture, which makes it a great addition to soups, stews and salads.

How to cook farro

Farro can be boiled until tender, similar to rice. Use one part farro to two parts water and simmer until tender. Cooked farro can also be added to soups and stews during cooking, as it tends to keep its chewy texture even when re-cooked.

FREEKEH

Freekeh is a high-fibre and high-protein cereal grain that is popular for adding texture to salads and soups. It is often made by roasting or drying and 'rubbing' green wheat, but other freekeh-style grains are becoming available. This process gives freekeh a unique taste and texture.

How to cook freekeh

Cook one part freekeh to 11/2 parts water. Simmer for around 15 minutes then take off the heat, cover and let stand. This will result in a fluffy-textured freekeh that makes a great substitute for rice. Freekeh can also be toasted and simmered with milk to create a wholesome porridge.

MILLET

Millet was once more widely consumed than rice. It is ability to grow in poor soils where other grains would not, means that it is still a staple in arid parts of India, Africa and Asia. It is also a great source of fibre and B vitamins, is low in fat, high in carbohydrates and is also gluten free.

How to cook millet

Millet can be cooked to a range of textures, depending on whether you want it fluffy or sticky. For fluffy millet, toast the grain in a pan for five minutes then add boiling water (we recommend one part millet to 21/4 parts water). For sticky millet, simmer one part millet in 23/4 parts water for around 15 minutes, then let stand for 10 minutes.

OATS

Porridge, muesli, granola – oats form the basis of some of our favourite foods. Oats are whole-grain, which means they still contain their fibrous bran and protein-rich germ. They are also rich in B vitamins and healthy fats, as well a soluble fibre called beta-glucan, which may reduce cholesterol levels.

How to cook oats

Most of us will be familiar with rolled oats (which are made from steamed and rolled oat groats), which can be eaten raw or cooked with milk or water to make porridge, or toasted for granola. Steel-cut oats are also popular; these are finely chopped oat groats, and can also be used to make porridge.

QUINOA

Like many pseudo-cereals, it is a great source of protein and essential amino acids, and is also rich in fibre and vitamins A and E. Originating in South America, quinoa has become a staple of the Western diet for all the right reasons.

How to cook quinoa

We recommend using two parts water to one part quinoa and simmering until the water has been absorbed. When cooked, the quinoa grains will have a small 'tail', which is the germ of the grain. Quinoa can also be added to soups and stews as it keeps its texture nicely, even when re-cooked.

BROWN RICE

Brown rice is a whole grain. It contains essential vitamins and minerals like magnesium, phosphorus, selenium, thiamine, niacin and vitamin B6, and is an excellent source of manganese. White rice, on the other hand, is milled to remove the husk and bran layers, leaving none of the goodness behind. The browner, the better.

How to cook rice

We suggest you use two parts water to one part rice. Add the rice to boiling water, then reduce to a simmer and cover the pot. Allow the rice to simmer for 15 to 25 minutes, or until most of the water has been absorbed. Turn off the heat and let it sit, covered, for 15 minutes.

Protein is important for optimum day-to-day functioning, feeling satiated and energised. Variety in protein source is required to ensure you are eating adequate amounts of protein with a plant-based diet, particularly when leading an active lifestyle.

— JACINTA SULTANA

Proteins

What is a 'complete' protein?

What is a 'complete' protein? A complete protein is a protein source that contains all nine essential amino acids, the building blocks of protein. These are required through dietary intake, as the body cannot generate them on its own. It is easy to achieve an adequate intake of amino acids by adding a variety of protein sources to your diet such as wholegrains, legumes, beans, nuts, seeds and plant-based protein powders.

Protein powders

Plant-based protein powders can be used to increase your intake of protein. They can be consumed on their own or added to smoothie bowls and baking recipes. Our new favourite is hemp, with an impressive fibre content and great ratio of healthy fats. We also enjoy rice proteins, particularly purple rice and pea protein.

---

[1]*Chia seeds – superfood or fad?,*
choice.com.au (July 2014)

Recommended serving sizes sourced through eatforhealth.gov.au (July 2015)

Protein volumes per 100g sourced through the USDA Food Composition Databases

SEEDS

Seeds are a source of healthy fats and vitamins. Chia seeds, in particular, are uniquely high in omega-3 and also contain high levels of calcium.[1] Other popular seeds include hemp, pepita, sesame and flaxseed (linseed). Most seeds contain around 18 grams of protein per 100 grams. The recommended serving size is 30 grams.

BEANS/LEGUMES

Beans and legumes are a source of fibre as well as protein. Popular higher protein choices include chickpeas (fava beans, 19 grams per 100 grams), edamame (young soy beans, 11 grams), black beans (21 grams), peanuts (25 grams) and lentils (9 grams). The recommended serving size is 150 grams.

SOY PRODUCTS

Soy products include tofu, tempeh and natto. Tofu is made from soy milk, and contains around 8 grams of protein per 100 grams, but is low in fibre. Fermented, whole-bean products such as tempeh and natto are more fibre rich, and contain around 18 grams per 100 grams.

NUTS

Nuts are a good source of healthy fats (being around 49 to 74 percent fat and nine to 20 percent protein). Popular nuts include almonds (21 grams per 100 grams), pistachios (20 grams), cashews (18 grams), hazelnuts (15 grams) and walnuts (15 grams). The recommended serving size is 30 grams.

NUTRITIONAL YEAST

Nutritional yeast is a great way to add a savoury, salty flavour to dishes – as well as extra protein. It is inactive, meaning it doesn't work as a leavening agent, and contains around 40 to 50 grams of protein per 100 grams. The recommended serving size is around 12 grams.

SPIRULINA

Spirulina powder will tint your food a brilliant shade of green, but this seaweed derivative is also high in protein. It contains around 57 grams of protein per 100 grams, and has a number of nutrients such as, calcium and magnesium. The recommended serving size is around 7 grams.

For people living a plant-based diet, there are many sources of calcium rich foods for us to enjoy like leafy vegetables, legumes, nuts and seeds. Almost all plant milks contain a similar amount of protein to cow's milk.

— JACINTA SULTANA

Milks

ALMOND MILK

Almonds are a great source of healthy fats, fibre and calcium. Naturally, they contain the highest amount of calcium compared with all nuts.

How to prepare Almond Milk

Almond milk is made by soaking whole almonds in water overnight and then blitzing the almonds with fresh water. We recommend blitzing the 1 cup of soaked almonds with 1 litre fresh drinking water. Sometimes this blended liquid is strained for a sediment-free milk. For the benefit of whole almonds, however, leave the sediment in and shake the milk before using.

COCONUT MILK

With a creamy texture and natural sweetness, it is easy to confuse coconut milk as being more naughty than nice. Be assured this is not the case! A liquid found naturally in coconut meat, it is capable of firing up your immune system and preventing illness. It also delivers a healthy dose of lauric acid, a medium-chain fatty acid used by the body for energy.

How to prepare Coconut Milk

Coconut milk is made by squeezing or pressing the white flesh of ripe coconuts, and can easily be made at home. However, it is more common to buy coconut milk in tins at the supermarket. Look for a product that contains no additives and a high percentage of coconut (some have water added).

SOY MILK

Soy milk is ultimately low in fat but contains some healthy polyunsaturated fat. It has a moderate amount of protein, carbohydrates, dietary fibre and calcium

How to prepare Soy Milk

Soy milk is made by soaking soybeans in water overnight and then blitzing the soybeans with fresh water. Again, it is a product many choose to buy. Look for a product with minimal additives as soy milk can contain sweeteners and thickeners.

RICE MILK

A light milk that can be quite sweet and is often made from brown rice and water. It is typically lower in protein, fat and calories, and higher in carbohydrates.

How to prepare Rice Milk

Rice milk is made by soaking rice in water overnight and then blitzing the rice with fresh water. To improve the nutrition available from the silky beverage, try consuming the whole milk without straining.

OAT MILK

Oat milk is another light milk that is higher in carbohydrates, lower in protein and contains a small amount of healthy unsaturated fats. When consumed with the oat sediment, oat milk contains a high amount of dietary fibre. Oats also contain important minerals, iron and magnesium.

How to prepare Oat Milk

Like rice milk, it is made by combining oats and water in a high-speed blender and processing to form a thin liquid.

Breakfast

CHAPTER 01

SMOOTHIE BOWLS - MUESLI - OATMEAL

Breakfast Bowls

Rise and shine. It is time to make yourself a happy little coconut.

Let's get your creative juices flowing, as the options here are endless. Happy, wholesome breakfasts are good for your soul and, as anyone following a healthy diet will tell you, the only limit here is your imagination.

When it comes to your plant-based breakfasts, smoothie bowls and oatmeals are your best friends. To start your day with a smile on your face, a spring in your step and a happy belly that is satisfied from dawn till dusk, wake up to a nourishing breakfast.

From velvety coconut cream rice puddings with warm spices, to refreshing açai smoothie bowls, breakfast is your time to shine. No matter where your mind wanders, your breakfast bowls can be topped with just about anything your heart desires.

Jazz up the humble oat, a timeless breakfast staple, with exciting recipes featuring sweet essences of nutmeg, cinnamon and maple syrup, topped with fresh fruit and nuts for that extra little bit of taste bud satisfaction.

This chapter features some of the most mouth-watering and tummy-tingling breakfasts you'll ever enjoy. Prepare to sparkle today with a breakfast that says good morning. After all, it is the most important meal you'll have today!

Go on, build your bowl, sprinkle on some superfoods and dig in.

Oh and by the way, if you're thinking about skipping breakfast, please don't. It is where the magic begins.

Sweet Potato Smoothie Bowl

Purple sweet potatoes (or ube yams) give this smoothie bowl a dreamy colour and wonderful depth of flavour. If you cannot find these at your local grocery store, feel free to use regular sweet potato (orange yams) – it will still taste just as delicious. You can even use the sweet potato mash from last night's dinner for your delicious morning smoothie bowl.

MAKES 1 BOWL

INGREDIENTS

Smoothie Bowl
- 1/2 cup purple (or regular) sweet potato, chopped
- 1 tablespoon almond butter
- 1/4 teaspoon cinnamon
- 1 1/2 frozen bananas
- 1/4 cup almond milk (or other plant-based milk)
- 1/2 teaspoon vanilla powder or vanilla extract

Toppings
- Cacao nibs
- Coconut flakes
- Cherries
- Mango
- Pumpkin seeds

METHOD

1. Steam your purple sweet potatoes for 15–20 minutes, or until tender.
2. Mash the steamed potatoes using a fork, then place in an airtight container in the freezer for 5–6 hours, preferably overnight.
3. Add the frozen purple sweet potato mash to a high-speed blender with all remaining ingredients, except for the toppings.
4. Blend until thick and creamy, adding more almond milk if needed.
5. Transfer to a Coconut Bowl and top with your desired toppings.

Caitlin Shoemaker @frommybowl
Caitlin is a recipe developer, content creator and life enthusiast. She is passionate about living a healthy, ethical, and mindful lifestyle and showing others how easy it can be. She grew up in Maryland and currently lives in Miami, Florida. Caitlin loves yoga and to start her day catching the morning sunrise. She also writes and is proud of how well she completes her epic 'to-do' lists.

Maple Coconut Soaked Oats

*Whoever said oats are boring has obviously never tried this recipe!
This delicious breakfast staple lets you be creative with your toppings
while being just as enjoyable as a basic soaked oats bowl.*

MAKES 1 BOWL

INGREDIENTS

- 1 cup rolled oats
- 1 tablespoon unsweetened coconut flakes
- 2 teaspoons pure maple syrup
- 1 teaspoon chia seeds
- Pinch of cinnamon
- 1 cup unsweetened almond milk
- 1 tablespoon nut butter of your choice
- Fresh fruit of your choice, to serve

METHOD

1. Combine oats, coconut, maple syrup, chia seeds and cinnamon in a bowl.
2. Add almond milk and mix thoroughly.
3. Allow to sit overnight or for at least 30 minutes in the refrigerator.
4. Top with nut butter and fresh fruit.

Candice Oliver @candicelynnfitvegan
Candice grew up in the deep-fried South, and from the age of 24 she's gradually eliminated all the unhealthy foods from her upbringing. Going vegan a number of years ago is the single best decision Candice has made. A plant-powered lifestyle, partnered with her passion for fitness, has Candice feeling the best she ever has.

Choc-Hazelnut Porridge with Grilled Banana

A nourishing and warming bowl of chocolatey goodness that tastes like dessert, yet is 100 percent good for you. Gooey caramelised grilled banana and crunchy hazelnuts make the perfect topping for this creamy chocolate porridge.

MAKES 1 BOWL

INGREDIENTS

- 1 ripe banana (or plantain)
- 1/2 cup brown rice flakes
- 2 teaspoons cacao or carob powder
- 1/2 tablespoon hazelnuts
- 1 Medjool date, chopped
- 1 cup plant milk of your choice
- 1/2 cup rolled oats
- 1/2 tablespoon tahini
- 1 teaspoon vanilla extract

METHOD

1. Combine oats and rice flakes in a pot with the plant milk, cacao, vanilla and chopped date, then simmer for 10–15 minutes, stirring until it thickens to your desired consistency.
2. While your porridge is cooking, peel and slice the banana and place the slices on a hot non-stick pan. Fry for about 1 minute, until golden, then flip and repeat for the other side. Be careful they don't burn.
3. Spoon your porridge into a Coconut Bowl, then top with the grilled banana slices, chopped hazelnuts and a drizzle of tahini.

Nina Gelbke @naturally_nina_
Nina is a Swiss-Australian nutritional and dietetic medicine student, passionate about all things to do with health, wellbeing and plant-based nutrition. She loves spending time outdoors, being active and creating delicious, wholesome plant-based recipes to share with the world.

Creamy Chocolate Tahini Oatmeal

Magical flavours of raw cocoa and tahini combined in one nutritious and satisfying breakfast bowl. This incredibly creamy oatmeal can be served hot or cold, and tastes delicious topped with fresh or frozen berries, pieces of vegan chocolate, or extra tahini and coconut flakes.

MAKES 1 BOWL

INGREDIENTS

Porridge
- 1/2 cup oats
- 2–3 dates (or 1 tablespoon maple syrup)
- 3/4 cup oat milk
- 1/2 cup water
- 1 tablespoon tahini
- 1 tablespoon raw cocoa powder
- Pinch of Himalayan salt

Toppings
- Vegan chocolate
- Berries
- Coconut flakes

METHOD

1. Combine the oats and dates with both liquids (oat milk and water) in a saucepan.
2. Leave the mixture to soak for 20–30 minutes.
3. Bring it slowly to the boil, then let it simmer on a very low heat until it thickens up, stirring frequently.
4. Add remaining porridge ingredients (tahini, cocoa powder and salt), and stir well before turning off the heat.
5. Refrigerate until cool, then give it a good stir. Add a splash of oat milk if it gets too thick while cooling down.
6. Transfer to your Coconut Bowl and top with berries and chocolate chunks.

Magda Tymczyj @oatmeal_stories
Magda is originally Polish, married to an Italian and lives in the Netherlands. Passionate about creating colourful, vegan meals that nourish both body and soul, Magda is also raising trilingual kids and teaching them a healthy, compassionate lifestyle, full of delicious plant-based foods.

Green Garden Smoothie Bowl

This pineapple-based green smoothie bowl makes a nourishing and satisfying breakfast with a tropical touch. Spinach and kale contain protein and a vast variety of micronutrients, making this meal the perfect post-workout treat to kickstart your day.

MAKES 2 BOWLS

INGREDIENTS

Smoothie Bowl
- 2 tablespoons coconut milk
- 1/2 cup coconut water
- 100g fresh or frozen kale
- 2 frozen bananas
- 100g frozen spinach
- 250g pineapple
- 1 tablespoon wheatgrass powder

Toppings
- Banana
- Berries
- Nuts of your choice

METHOD

1. Put all smoothie ingredients into a high-speed blender.
2. Blend on medium–high speed for 60 seconds or until the smoothie is completely smooth and no thick pieces are visible anymore.
3. Transfer to your Coconut Bowls and add your toppings.

Laura Grosch @laurafruitfairy
Laura's the fruit fairy from South Germany who fell in love with nature at an early age and regularly goes for forest walks and hikes. She is a passionate healthy lifestyle and food blogger (fruit-fairy.com) who loves to discover the world and has already lived abroad in the UK, Serbia and China.

Golden Granola Bowl

This homemade granola recipe is as versatile as it is tasty. You can use it to sprinkle on your smoothie bowl, or as the main event for a fulfilling start to your day. Make it in a big batch and use it any way you please. Make it in a batch of 1kg and use approx 100g as the base of your breakfast bowl.

MAKES 1KG

INGREDIENTS

- 100g walnuts, chopped
- 100g pumpkin seeds
- 500g oats
- 200g popped quinoa
- 70g coconut sugar syrup
- 2 teaspoons cinnamon

METHOD

1. Toast the walnuts, pumpkin seeds, oats and popped quinoa in a non-stick pan on medium heat.
2. Once the ingredients have turned slightly brown turn down the heat to low.
3. Add the coconut sugar syrup and the cinnamon and mix, continue toasting until your granola is golden.
4. Turn the heat off and let the granola cool down, either in the pan or on a piece of baking paper.
5. Add 100g to your coconut bowl, top with 1 banana and your desired amount of coconut, almond or oat milk.

Damian Wachsmann @highcarbguru
Damian is a vegan food blogger and nutrition student from Gießen, Germany. Through social media and his blog highcarbguru.com, Damian shares simple and healthy recipes to show you how easy it is to follow a healthy diet, and how to stick to it for the long term.

Oahu's North Shore Smoothie Bowl

This is my go-to snack every day after the beach. It is the perfect way to refuel and refresh. I always have açai in the freezer so I can make bowls for all the keiki (kids) and friends that stop by.

MAKES 2 BOWLS

INGREDIENTS

- 200g frozen açai
- 3 frozen bananas
- 1/2 cup frozen blueberries
- 1/2 cup frozen mango
- Dash of almond milk

METHOD

1. Blend all ingredients on medium until they have been broken down. Using the tamper stick, turn blender to high. Blend and mix until thick and smooth.
2. Serve in your Coconut Bowls and enjoy.

Tip: Top your smoothie bowls with whatever makes you happy! The Earthy Andy family enjoys a good granola, coconut flakes, fresh juicy fruit and, sometimes, peanut butter or chocolate.

Andy Hannemann @earthyandy
Andy is mamma to two littlies living on the North Shore of Oahu, while working as a brand consultant for a sunscreen company. She has a passion for the outdoors, good food and good people. To Andy that is the recipe for a good life and if you can be on the beach along the way then all the better! For endless good vibes visit @earthyandy or earthyandy.com

Chocolate Pudding Breakfast Oatmeal

A deliciously creamy combination of chocolate pudding and nutrient-dense oatmeal that provides you with a tasty and satisfying start to your day.

MAKES 2 BOWLS

INGREDIENTS

Oatmeal
- 1 cup (or 100g) oats
- 40g vegan chocolate custard or pudding powder
- 2 dates or 2 teaspoons maple syrup
- 500ml liquid (a mixture of water and any kind of plant-based milk)
- Cinnamon (optional)

Toppings
- As desired; my favourites are banana, frozen berries and granola

METHOD

1. In a jar, combine the vegan custard powder, dates and a splash of water. Close the jar with a lid and shake well until the powder has dissolved, adding more water if required.
2. Heat up the remaining amount of plant milk and water on a stove until it boils.
3. Add in the mixture from the jar, stir well and simmer.
4. Lower the heat and add in the oats and cinnamon. Stir until even and remove the pot from the heat to let the oats absorb the liquid.
5. Leave overnight in the fridge or for at least 30 minutes.
6. Pour into your Coconut Bowls. For extra flavour, add a pinch of cinnamon.

Tip: For the most intense flavour and optimal texture, prepare this the night before and let it sit until breakfast time.

Vera Adams @datesandfigs

Vera is a breakfast enthusiast from Germany. She's passionate about living a healthy and happy vegan life surrounded by healthy and happy people. Vera loves to create delicious and nutritious cruelty-free treats and meals that everyone can enjoy.

Strawberry Vanilla Chia Pudding Bowl

Chia pudding is a breakfast favourite and this tasty take on it is a real winner. The strawberry and vanilla combo gives you that little bit of sweetness that you're after in the morning, while the chia pudding will keep you feeling full until you're ready for lunch.

MAKES 2 BOWLS

INGREDIENTS

Chia Pudding
- 4 tablespoons chia seeds
- 1 1/2 cups almond milk
- 2 teaspoons vanilla extract
- 1/2 cup strawberries

Toppings
- Strawberries
- White chocolate
  or dark chocolate
- Coconut flakes

METHOD

1. Stir chia seeds, almond milk and vanilla together well in a jar or bowl. Leave it to thicken for at least 30 minutes (or even overnight) stirring at least once.
2. Before serving, mash strawberries in a bowl and add half the chia pudding. Mix well to incorporate, then layer up into bowls.
3. Add topping with vegan white chocolate (or dark chocolate), strawberries and coconut flakes.

Tip: One of the best things about chia puddings is that you can add whatever you really like as a topping. Be as creative and adventurous as you like. However, I think 3–4 toppings is the perfect amount to complement the taste of your chia pudding.

Harriet Porterfield @bos.kitchen
Harriet would like to welcome you to her kitchen @bos.kitchen. She's a cat-loving, herbal tea-hoarding foodie from the UK with a passion for plant-based food. Her blog, boskitchen.com, inspires you to try more plant-based meals.

Piña Colada Oatmeal

This oatmeal recipe tastes more like a cocktail than breakfast,
yet is an incredibly nutritious way to start your day.

MAKES 2 BOWLS

INGREDIENTS

Oatmeal
- 1 cup water
- 1 cup coconut milk
- 1 cup oats
- 1–2 teaspoons shredded coconut
- 1 teaspoon coconut sugar (optional)

Toppings
- Fresh or dried pineapple
- Toasted coconut
- Almonds

METHOD

1. In a small pot, bring water and coconut milk to a boil. Once boiling add in the oats, turn heat down to medium and stir constantly (makes it creamier).
2. While stirring, add in shredded coconut and coconut sugar (if using).
3. Cook until liquid is absorbed and the oats are creamy.
4. Optional to cool in the refrigerator or enjoy warm.
5. When you're ready, transfer into your Coconut Bowls, then add pineapple, toasted coconut and flaked almonds.

Alina Zänglein @plantbasedali_
Alina hails from Germany and loves to travel the world. She began her vegan lifestyle in 2015 while recovering from an eating disorder. Upon discovering healthy and yummy vegan food, she began to share her story, recipes and inspiration with people on social media.

Choc-Hazelnut Overnight Oats

Chocolate addicts will love this vegan overnight oat recipe. Equally as healthy as it is scrumptious, this brekkie could be mistaken for dessert.

MAKES 1 BOWL

INGREDIENTS

- 2 tablespoons cacao nibs
- 2 tablespoons cacao powder
- 1 tablespoon chia seeds
- 1 tablespoon maple syrup (optional, to taste
- 1/4 cup hazelnut butter (almond butter works well too)
- 1/2 cup rolled oats
- 1/2 cup quick oats
- 1 cup non-dairy milk
- Pinch of sea salt

METHOD

1. The night before, mix all the ingredients in a jar.
2. Add the maple syrup to taste and refrigerate overnight.
3. The next morning, give it a quick stir and serve in your Coconut Bowl with your favorite toppings. You could also simply bring the jar with you and eat it on your way to work.

Odile Joly-Petit @odilejp
Odile is a French-Canadian vegan food photographer and blogger who now lives in the Netherlands. Through her food photography, Odile aspires to inspire by showing you why cooking and eating vegan food is an amazing decision.

Salted Caramel Smoothie Bowl

A salted caramel smoothie bowl is the perfect healthy option for those who crave something sweet to start the day. You'll be amazed at the vegan salted caramel flavours from this recipe.

MAKES 2 BOWLS

INGREDIENTS

Smoothie Bowls
- 4 frozen bananas
- 6 Medjool dates
- 1/2 cup coconut cream
- 1 tablespoon cashew butter
- Pinch of salt
- Pinch of cinnamon
- 1/2 cup water
- 1 teaspoon maca powder

Toppings
- Whatever your heart desires

METHOD

1. Put all ingredients into a high-speed blender and mix until smooth.
2. Pour the smoothie into your Coconut Bowls and top with your favourite fruits and more cashew butter.

Agata Biernat @cinnamonandberries
Agata is a young passionate vegan from Poland. She loves living a healthy vegan lifestyle and creating delicious vegan recipes that everyone can enjoy. It is impossible for Agata to go a day without a smoothie bowl.

Tropical Lilikoi & Cookie Dough Smoothie Bowl

This breakfast smoothie bowl is even tastier than it sounds. The tropical flavours of the smoothie bowl, topped with the guilt-free cookie dough, will have you craving more for lunch, dinner and dessert.

MAKES 2 BOWLS + EXTRA COOKIE DOUGH

INGREDIENTS

High Protein Cookie Dough
- 1/2 cup oats
- 1 1/2 cups chickpeas, rinsed
- 1 teaspoon coconut oil
- 2 teaspoon coconut sugar
- 6 dates
- 1 tablespoon flaxseed meal
- 1 tablespoon peanut butter
- Pinch of salt
- Pinch of fresh vanilla
- 50g dark chocolate

Smoothie Bowl Base
- 3 frozen bananas, chopped
- 1/2 teaspoon cinnamon
- 1/4 cup coconut milk
- 1/2 passion fruit
- 1 teaspoon peanut butter
- 1 teaspoon vanilla, freshly grated

Suggested Toppings
- Banana, cacao nibs, coconut chips, peanut butter and remaining half of passion fruit

METHOD

1. In a high-speed blender, add the oats and process into flour.
2. Then add all remaining cookie dough ingredients, except chocolate. Blend until it forms a dough.
3. Pour into a bowl, add chocolate chunks and combine. You can make balls, bars or cookie shapes out of it, and you can even cook it.
4. Store in an air-tight container in the fridge for a few days.
5. Add all smoothie bowl base ingredients to a high-speed blender. Blend until it forms a thick and smooth consistency.
6. Pour smoothie into your Coconut Bowls, decorate with suggested toppings or sprinkle on whatever you like.

Amélie Balland @amelietahiti
Amélie is a vegan blogger and YouTuber from Tahiti, now living in France. She calls her vegan transition a health, ethical and environmental awakening, and loves to share her healthy vegan lifestyle and passion for nutrition, fitness and helping others. Amélie is a travel enthusiast and loves anything active – dance, surf, yoga, fitness, hiking, you name it.

Nourishing Rice Porridge

This recipe brings dessert to breakfast time (in a healthy way, of course) and is allergy friendly. It makes a warm bowl of what tastes like a creamy rice pudding, topped with creamy tahini, chia seeds and coconut sugar. Health is not compromised with this delicious bowl. It contains an impressive fibre content plus a balance of protein and omega fatty acids.

MAKES 2 BOWLS

INGREDIENTS

- 1 cup brown rice flakes
- 1 1/2 cups almond milk
- 1 tablespoon chia seeds
- 1 tablespoon coconut sugar
- 1 tablespoon tahini
- 4 strawberries, sliced

METHOD

1. Place the brown rice flakes and almond milk in a pot on the stove over a medium heat.
2. Bring to a simmer and allow the brown rice flakes to soften until almond milk is absorbed and it becomes a creamy texture.
3. Remove from heat and pour into a bowl, then top with chia seeds, coconut sugar and tahini.
4. Pour the rice pudding into your Coconut Bowls and top with strawberries.

Jacinta Sultana @jacinta_sultana
Jacinta is a vegan dietitian based on the Sunshine Coast, Australia. She is passionate about helping people to be the healthiest and happiest versions of themselves, no matter where they are on their journey. Jacinta loves sharing her nutritional knowledge with others to live the most indulgent plant-based lifestyle.

Dragon Fruit Breakfast Bowl

This delicious breakfast recipe takes only a couple of minutes to prepare, yet will leave you thinking about it all day long. The coconut yoghurt and dragon fruit complement each other so well, while the toppings give you another burst of delicious flavours.

MAKES 2 BOWLS

INGREDIENTS

- 1 pink dragon fruit
- 4 cups coconut yoghurt
- 1 cup granola
- 2 kiwifruit
- 2 tablespoons coconut flakes

METHOD

1. Mash pink dragon fruit in a bowl.
2. Add coconut yoghurt to the bowl and mix.
3. Scoop into your Coconut Bowls and top with granola, kiwifruit and coconut flakes.

Olia Saunders @ps.ny
Olia is a photographer and artist based in New York City. Originally from St. Petersburg, Russia, Olia has also lived in Germany and Italy. Her experiences as a student abroad led to her adopting a plant-based diet, and her passion for a holistic lifestyle and vegan cooking remain strong. One look at Olia's Instagram feed will have you falling in love with her toy poodle, Cookie.

Ultimate Açai Bowl

Kick start your day the perfect way with the ultimate açai bowl. This fruity delight is a daily go-to for many health enthusiasts as it is packed with vitamins, minerals, antioxidants and energy to keep you satisfied and nourished until lunch time. Most importantly, though, it tastes super-duper delicious!

MAKES 2 BOWLS

INGREDIENTS

Bowl
- 250ml watermelon juice (blended watermelon with a dash of water) or coconut water
- 200g frozen açai
- 1 fresh banana
- 1 frozen banana
- 1/2 cup frozen blueberries
- 1 cup frozen mango chunks
- 1 tablespoon chia seeds

Toppings
- Chosen by you

METHOD

1. Add the liquid of choice, açai, banana, blueberries, mango and chia seeds to a high-speed blender.
2. Blend until smooth and thick. If your blender has a tamper tool, push down the ingredients to help combine. Add more liquid if required.
3. Spoon into your Coconut Bowls and top with your favourite goodies, such as fruits, coconut, goji berries, chia seeds, cacao nibs, chocolate sauce and edible flowers.

Tess Begg @tessbegg
Tess is a Sydney-based vegan, foodie and fitness enthusiast. She inspires people globally to live a happy, healthy and active lifestyle through her Instagram and YouTube channels, sharing hundreds of 'What I Eat in a Day' videos, workouts, delicious recipes and posts that promote veganism as an abundant lifestyle with endless cruelty-free options.

Green Power Smoothie Bowl

A simple combination of frozen bananas, mango, avocado and superfoods makes this smoothie a highly nutritious and energy-boosting breakfast. Avocado gives it a smooth and creamy texture and provides you with a daily dose of healthy fats. This smoothie will keep you satisfied and feeling good for hours.

MAKES 2 BOWLS

INGREDIENTS

Smoothie Bowl

- 3 frozen bananas, chopped
- 1 small mango, diced and frozen
- 1/2 avocado
- 2 tablespoons hemp seeds
- 1 handful spinach
- 1/2 teaspoon spirulina powder
- 1 teaspoon maca powder

Toppings

- Your own selection of goodies

METHOD

1. Put frozen bananas and mango in the blender and blend on high speed until you get a creamy texture.
2. Add avocado, hemp seeds, spinach, spirulina and maca powder. Blend on high speed until completely smooth and creamy.
3. Serve in your Coconut Bowls and top with a sprinkle of white sesame seeds and chia seeds, frozen berries and edible flowers.

Nensi & Slaven Beram @alltheworldisgreen
Nensi and Slaven are from Croatia and are very passionate about vegan food and food photography. They absolutely love cooking, discovering and trying new recipes and ingredients, and sharing their experiences on their blog (rainbowinmykitchen.com) and on social media. Their goal is to be inspired and to inspire other people to live a healthier life.

Homemade Rawnola Cereal

A homemade, versatile recipe for a quick, nutritious meal at any time of the day. Plus, you can say that you made your very own epic rawnola including the milk, from scratch!

MAKES 5 BOWLS

INGREDIENTS

Rawnola
- 1 cup pitted dates
- 1 cup raw rolled oats
- 1 cup dried coconut
- 1 tablespoon pure maple syrup or brown rice malt syrup (optional, this makes it stickier if the recipe is dry)
- 1/4 cup of raw vegan chocolate (if you would like to make a chocolate version)

Toppings
- Berries, desired amount
- Almond milk (see recipe page 256)

METHOD

1. Using your high-speed blender, add all ingredients except for maple syrup.
2. Blend and pulse until desired consistency is achieved. If you are making the chocolate version, add1/4cup raw vegan chocolate.
3. When combined well, slowly drizzle a small amount of maple syrup while pulsing. Remember, this sweetener is optional. It helps make the rawnola stickier.
4. Store in a glass jar in the fridge for 2 weeks. Although, I'd be very surprised if you can keep this stuff in your fridge that long without eating it all.
5. Add the rawnola to your Coconut Bowls, then top with fresh berries such as blackberries and blueberries.
6. Pour the almond milk on top and you have yourself your own vegan homemade cereal that tastes seriously epic, and you just made it from scratch with little effort!

Tip: This will make a 1-litre mason jar. You can halve the recipe if you want a smaller batch jar.

Loni Jane @lonijane
Loni is a pioneer plant-based Instagram influencer, creator of the famous #rawnola and author of e-books *Feel the Lean 1.0* and *2.0.* Mum of two plant-powered kids and living on the great southern land, Australia. Loni is about all things plant-based: health, healing, learning, teaching, nature and love.

Spiced Oatmeal

*This breakfast is warm and creamy with just the right amount of spice.
Not to mention, it'll keep you satisfied all morning. Pair with your favourite
fresh fruit and nuts and you're left with a healthy and delicious breakfast
to keep you going all day.*

MAKES 1 BOWL

INGREDIENTS

Oatmeal

- 1 cup coconut milk
- 1 teaspoon ground cinnamon
- 1/2 teaspoon ground ginger
- 1/2 teaspoon ground nutmeg
- 1/2 teaspoon ground cloves
- 1/8 teaspoon ground cardamom
- 1 tablespoon maple syrup
- 1 cup oats
- 1 teaspoon vanilla extract
- 1 cup water

Toppings

- Fresh fruit
- Nuts
- Seeds

METHOD

1. Put all ingredients into a small saucepan on medium heat.
2. Simmer, stirring frequently, until you reach your desired consistency.
3. Pour into your Coconut Bowl and top with ingredients of choice.

Cherie Tu @thrivingonplants
Cherie is from Sydney, Australia, and has never looked back since discovering veganism when
she was 15 years old. Cherie is extremely passionate about plant-based cooking, nutrition and
fitness and loves sharing her journey online with people from all around the world, hoping to
inspire and help others.

Tropical Açai Smoothie Bowl

Smoothie bowls are essential to a happy, healthy diet. They're so versatile and can satisfy any craving, whether you're after a refreshing breakfast, midday snack or a sweet-yet-healthy dessert. This easy recipe is a favourite of mine – it is super yummy and fun to eat out of my Coconut Bowl.

MAKES 2 BOWLS

INGREDIENTS

- 1 banana, peeled and frozen
- 1 cup pineapple, cubed and frozen
- 100g frozen açai berries
- 1 tablespoon hemp seeds
- 1/2 cup almond milk (see recipe page 256)

METHOD

1. Pop all ingredients into a high-speed blender and mix until thick and creamy.
2. Pour into your Coconut Bowls, top with something crunchy and serve.

Yovana Mendoza @rawvana
Yovana is a Mexican-American vegan blogger who promotes practising daily gratitude and self love. Creator of the Rawvana lifestyle – which is about connecting your body, mind and spirit by creating harmony between yourself, your thoughts and the world – Yovana believes that true beauty comes from within. She wants to help you feel amazing, because when you feel amazing, you look amazing.

Creamy Coconut Rice Pudding with Mango Sauce

This amazing rice pudding recipe will transfer you to the tropics with its delicious coconut flavour topped with tasty mango sauce. The sauce can be substituted with other fruits for a versatile breakfast staple.

MAKES 2 BOWLS

INGREDIENTS

Rice Pudding
- 1 cup jasmine rice or basmati rice
- 2 cups water or plant milk
- 1 cup coconut milk (full-fat)
- 1–2 teaspoons coconut sugar
- 1 teaspoon coconut oil
- 1 teaspoon coconut butter (optional)
- Pinch of vanilla or 1/2 teaspoon vanilla extract

Mango Sauce
- 1 ripe mango

METHOD

1. Put the rice in a saucepan together with plant-based milk, coconut milk and coconut sugar. Bring to the boil, cover and then simmer on a very low temperature for about 15 minutes. Stir occasionally.
2. While the rice is cooking, peel the mango, cut it in pieces and place in a high-speed blender. Mix until you get a smooth and creamy consistency.
3. Remove the rice from the heat, add coconut oil and coconut butter.
4. Mix the rice in the saucepan with a stick blender until you get a smooth texture. If necessary add a little bit more liquid, depending on the desired consistency.
5. Pour the rice pudding into your Coconut Bowls and top it with the mango sauce and fresh fruits of your choice.

Conny Lutze @plantbased_food_and_travel
Conny is a passionate foodie who wants to show you how easy it is to live a vegan lifestyle. As someone who has experienced an eating disorder and many food intolerances, Conny believes that going vegan is the best decision that she ever made. She creates many recipes with simple ingredients that are free from refined sugar and soy, and most of her recipes are also gluten free.

Light Bowls

CHAPTER 02

SALADS - SOUPS - WRAPS

Light Bowls

Like a kid in a candy store, the meals in this chapter are what your dreams are made of.

Eat your way through the colours of the rainbow with recipes from this section – opting for something lighter doesn't have to mean sacrificing flavour. Enjoy a delicious buddha bowl filled with greens, grains and proteins. Slurp up heart-warming soups or munch on a wrap filled with almighty goodness. These meals will have you feeling recharged and radiating good vibes all day long.

When it comes to light meals, don't underestimate the power of plants. For a low carb meal that will leave you feeling fresh and fabulous, use lettuce for wraps, rice paper for rolls, and zoodles (zucchini noodles) instead of pasta.

If it is a healthy bite on the go that you're after, let's get you glowing with a roll filled with as much colour as flavour. Be inspired by every shade of nature, with veggies stacked with vitamins and minerals, all rolled up into one yummy lunch.

For something a little larger, a veggie soup will do the trick, and it is the perfect way to let your imagination off the leash with so many flavours at your fingertips. Cradle your Coconut Bowl with two hands and let the heat of a hearty soup warm you from the inside out.

There are no rules here; be inventive, mix and match. Treat your Coconut Bowl like a blank canvas. You've got this.

Green Garden Bowl with Alfredo Pesto Pasta

These beautiful green bowls are packed with delicious flavours and nutrients. Creamy alfredo pasta is a family favourite, which will get your taste buds dancing as you dive into the vibrant garden greens. Fresh basil pesto complements the meal nicely with an extra burst of flavour.

MAKES 4 BOWLS

INGREDIENTS

Pasta
- 4 cups brown rice spirals
- 1 1/2 cups raw cashew nuts
- 2 tablespoons capers
- 3/4 cup rice milk
- 2 tablespoon nutritional yeast
- 1 tablespoon sesame seeds

Greens
- 3 cups organic frozen peas
- 3 cups sunflower or pea sprouts
- 1 lebanese cucumber, sliced into long strips and rolled

Pesto
- 6 cups fresh basil leaves
- 2 cloves garlic
- Juice of 1 lemon
- 1/3 cup macadamia nuts
- 1/4 cup nutritional yeast
- 1/2 cup olive oil
- 1/4 cup pine nuts

METHOD

Pasta & Greens
1. Place the cashews into a small bowl and fill with warm water until well covered. Soak for 8 hours. Alternatively, soak in boiled water for at least one hour until soft.
2. Bring two pots of water to the boil. Once boiling, place the brown rice spirals and frozen peas into the two separate pots. Stir gently and continue to boil the peas for approximately 4 minutes and the spirals for 8–10 minutes, until soft.
3. Place the prepared cashews, capers, rice milk and nutritional yeast in a high-speed blender and blend until smooth.
4. Drain the spirals and rinse under warm running water for 30 seconds. Then, pour into the prepared alfredo sauce and mix well.
5. Half fill four Coconut Bowls with alfredo pasta and top with raw sesame seeds. Next, place the green peas and sprouts evenly into the remaining half of the bowls.
6. Place cucumber rolls evenly into the centre of each bowl.

Pesto
7. Place all ingredients in a high-speed blender and blend until smooth.
8. Add a dollop of pesto into each Coconut Bowl to garnish your meal.
9. Store any remaining pesto in an airtight jar. Place in the fridge and keep for up to 5 days.

Sophie Steevens @rawandfree
Sophie is from Raw and Free, a health blog and website dedicated to sharing her passion for living a healthy, sustainable plant-based lifestyle, while helping others to do the same. Originally from New Zealand and now based on the Gold Coast, Australia, with her partner and two beautiful boys.

Red Sprouted Superfood Salad

This red sprouted superfood salad is packed with flavour, nutrients, enzymes and antioxidants. It can easily be served as a main dish or as a side. Unlike some salads, even the dressing adds to the nutritional value of this dish as it contains two superfood ingredients: pomegranates and açai. The pomegranate adds a subtle sweetness which perfectly balances the bitterness of the açai, while the maple roasted walnuts add a delicious crunch.

MAKES 2 BOWLS

INGREDIENTS

Salad

- 1 cup cooked red quinoa
- 1 tablespoon olive oil
- 1 red onion, finely sliced
- 1 tablespoon ginger, grated
- 2 cups red cabbage, shredded
- 1 beetroot, peeled and spiralised
- 1 cup sorrel leaves
- 1 cup sunflower sprouts
- 1 cup mung bean sprouts
- 6 radishes, sliced
- 1 ripe avocado, sliced

Maple Roasted Walnuts

- 1/2 cup activated walnuts
- 1 tablespoon maple syrup
- 1 teaspoon coconut oil

Dressing

- 1 tablespoon pomegranates
- 2 tablespoons olive oil
- 1/2 teaspoon açai powder
- 1/4 cup fresh lemon juice
- 1/4 teaspoon Himalayan salt

METHOD

1. Cook quinoa as per instructions of your chosen brand.
2. Saute onion in olive oil for a few minutes or until soft and slightly crispy, taking care not to burn.
3. Once onion has softened, add quinoa and grated ginger, stir and then allow to cool completely.
4. Meanwhile, prepare maple roasted walnuts.
5. Combine all ingredients in a non-stick pan and cook over low heat for approx. 5 minutes, stirring constantly and then set aside.
6. To make dressing, simply combine all ingredients in a small dish and mix well.
7. Add cabbage, beetroot, sorrel leaves, sprouts and radish to quinoa mixture and toss salad in the dressing.
8. Transfer salad to your Coconut Bowls and garnish with maple roasted walnuts, avocado, your choice of additional sprouts (optional), salt and pepper.

Hannah Singleton & Jennifer Murrant @healthyluxe
Health Synergy is a mother-daughter team that evolved from a shared love and appreciation for health, wellness and travel. Their philosophy on food is using ingredients that are as close to their natural source as possible, organic, seasonal and nutrient dense. All their recipes are refined sugar free, most are gluten free, and there is an abundance of vegan options.

Summer Veggie Rainbow Rolls

These wraps are perfect to take with you for lunch on the go. They are light and fresh, yet filling and satisfying at the same time. Colourful food is so much fun to eat, not to mention the abundance of vitamins and minerals that go hand-in-hand with eating the rainbow. They are also quick to make – it couldn't be easier, just chop, roll and go!

MAKES 2 LARGE WRAPS

INGREDIENTS

Hummus
- 1 red capsicum, halved
- 1 1/2 cups of chickpeas, rinsed and drained
- 1 tablespoon olive oil
- 1 clove garlic
- 1 tablespoon lemon juice
- Pinch of sea salt
- 1 tablespoon tahini

Veggie Rolls
- 2 wholemeal wraps
- 1/3 cucumber, sliced
- 2 carrots, grated
- 1 cup red cabbage, sliced
- 1 red capsicum, sliced
- 1 cup spinach
- 1/2 handful fresh tarragon

METHOD

Hummus
1. Place capsicum halves on a baking tray lined with baking paper. Place into the oven pre-heated at 200°C and roast for 15–20 minutes. Set aside to cool.
2. Blend the chickpeas, olive oil, garlic, lemon juice, salt and tahini. Add a few tablespoons of water if needed. Blend until smooth. Add baked capsicum and blend again, until smooth.

Veggie Rolls
3. Lay the wraps on a sheet of baking paper. Spread a generous helping of hummus on each wrap.
4. Layer up all the veggies and roll up the wraps tightly. Secure each wrap by tying a piece of string around it.

Christina Leopold @addictedtodates
Christina is a vegan food blogger from south west Ireland. Every spare minute she has goes into her passions of creating recipes and food photography. One day she hopes to open a raw cake bar, quite possibly overseas. Christina loves listening to music to get the creative juices flowing – no recipe is created without Pearl Jam, Tool or Sound Garden blaring in the background.

Rainbow Nourishment Bowl

This rainbow bowl does exactly what the name suggests; it nourishes your body with a bunch of delicious and colourful ingredients. Often ingredients of the same colour share similar vitamins and nutrients, so a bowl with all the colours of the rainbow will always fuel you with a variety of health benefits. This bowl looks so pretty, almost too beautiful to eat (but I recommend you do).

MAKES 2 BOWLS

INGREDIENTS

- 2 cups spinach
- 1/2 cup corn kernels (fresh from a cob if possible)
- 1/2 cup edamame beans
- 1/2 cup cabbage, shredded
- 1/4 cup carrots, sliced
- 1/2 cup quinoa, cooked
- 1 radish, sliced
- Handful pea shoot sprouts (or other type of sprouts)
- 1/2 avocado, sliced
- Sesame seeds
- Juice of 1/2 lemon

METHOD

1. Start by filling the bottom of the Coconut Bowls with spinach.
2. Place the corn, edamame, cabbage, carrots, quinoa (cooked), radish, sprouts, and avocado in small piles on top of the bowls.
3. Sprinkle with sesame seeds.
4. Dress with some lemon juice if desired (or any dressing you like).

Jessica Hoffman @choosingchia
Jess is a wholesome and healthy living blogger from Canada. Her blog, choosingchia.com, is packed with healthy recipes and shows you that eating clean does not mean limiting yourself to a plate of lettuce and almonds. Her philosophy is simple: Eat more plants, eat locally when you can, and focus on fresh and seasonal ingredients.

Avocado Pesto Pasta

*A modern twist on a classic dish, and also a very healthy, nourishing
way to get your glow on with your daily dose of greens.*

MAKES 2 BOWLS

INGREDIENTS

Pesto

- 3 packed cups fresh greens
  of your choice (basil, kale,
  spinach, etc.)
- A few handfuls of bitter herbs
  (rocket, coriander, etc.)
- 1/2 cup nuts of your choice
  (I opt for equal amounts
  of cashews, pine nuts and
  pistachios)
- 1/4 cup organic olive oil
- 1/2 cup nutritional yeast
- Juice of 1 lemon
- 1 clove garlic, minced

Pasta

- 1 avocado
- 250g spiral pasta
- 1 tablespoon vegan butter
- 1/4 cup pistachios, chopped,
  to garnish
- Fresh herbs, to garnish
- Salt and pepper to taste

METHOD

1. In a high-speed blender, add all pesto ingredients and process until the
   mixture is combined but still has a slightly chunky texture.
2. Mash avocado into a bowl with a fork. Add pesto and stir to combine.
   Season to taste.
3. Cook pasta in a pot of boiling, salted water. Drain and stir through
   vegan butter and pesto until the pasta is evenly coated.
4. Serve in your Coconut Bowls and top with pistachios, fresh herbs
   of choice, salt and freshly cracked pepper.

Jovi Fawn @earthfawn
Jovi is a passionate, plant-based foodie who loves to test the boundaries with her vegan
cooking. She thrives in the rawness and realness of life and enjoys practising spending each
day living in the present moment. She currently resides in the Australian subtropics and tries
to use Mother Nature as much as possible as her inspiration.

Raw Rainbow Salad with Avocado Mango Dressing

This delicious raw vegan rainbow salad is as tasty as it is colourful, but it is the avocado mango dressing that steals the limelight. Both sweet and refreshing, this will become a regular for you during summer.

MAKES 3 BOWLS

INGREDIENTS

Rainbow Salad

- 2 carrots, sliced into ribbons
- 3 cucumbers, sliced
- 2 red capsicums, diced
- 1 mango, diced
- 1/4 red cabbage, sliced
- Handful of edible butterfly pea flowers (optional)

For the Dressing

- 2–3 spring onions
- 2 avocados
- 1 mango
- Juice of 1–2 limes
- 2 cloves garlic
- 1/2 teaspoon cumin
- Salt and pepper

METHOD

1. Arrange the veggies and fruit side by side into your Coconut Bowls to resemble a rainbow (it tastes better when you do this).
2. Blend all the dressing ingredients in a high-speed blender until completely smooth.
3. Pour the dressing over your rainbow salad.

Michaela Vais @elavegan
Michaela has been vegan since 2011 and loves to eat healthy plant-based meals. She prepares a huge raw rainbow salad for lunch every single day, but also loves making sweets like brownies and cakes as healthy as possible, and she shares all her recipes on her blog elavegan.com. Originally from Germany, Michaela and her partner moved to the Caribbean, where they live together with their rescue cat, Ginger.

Veggies with Roasted Capsicum Hummus

This savoury bowl of goodness is sure to impress, with homemade roasted capsicum hummus the star of the show. A family favourite, this dish is best served with a variety of nutrient-packed raw or cooked veggies of your choice. Stir together into buddha bowls or serve separately as veggie dippers.

MAKES 4–6 BOWLS

INGREDIENTS

Buddha Bowl or Veggie Dippers
- 1kg golden potatoes, cut into 1.5cm-thick chips
- 500g sweet potatoes, cut into 1.5cm-thick chips
- Garlic powder
- Black pepper

Hummus
- 500g potatoes, diced
- 1 red capsicum, sliced
- 1/2 onion, sliced
- 1 1/2 cup chickpeas, rinsed
- 1 teaspoon paprika
- 1 teaspoon garlic powder
- 1/4 cup pickled jalapeños
- 4 tablespoons lemon juice
- 1/2 cup water
- 2 tablespoons tahini

To Serve
- Vegetables of your choice, cooked or raw

METHOD

1. Boil potatoes for the hummus until cooked. Drain and set aside.
2. Pre-heat oven to 180°C. Line a baking tray with baking paper and arrange golden and sweet potato chips on tray. Sprinkle over garlic powder and black pepper and bake for 40–50 minutes. Set aside.
3. Make a start on the hummus by sauteing the capsicum and onion in a pan with a little water on medium heat. Stir occasionally and add water if veggies start to stick to pan.
4. In a high-speed blender, blend chickpeas on high with paprika, garlic powder, pickled jalapeños, lemon juice, water, 1 cup of the boiled potatoes and 1 cup of the sauteed capsicum and onion mixture. Blend until chunky and well combined.
5. Serve all the veggies in Coconut Bowls topped with hummus. Stir together or serve separately as dips.

Ellen Fisher @ellenfisher

Ellen is a mother, wife and lover of life. She lives in Maui, Hawaii with her boys, sharing her passion for living an eco-conscious lifestyle. Ellen's greatest joys and passions include getting outdoors to explore nature, raising healthy children through a compassionate vegan lifestyle, breastfeeding, home birthing and gentle parenting. All of these activities uplift her soul, which is why she loves sharing them with the world.

Quinoa Superfood Salad

A quinoa salad is not just a quinoa salad, as you can serve it so many different ways. This quinoa superfood salad bowl is not only vibrant and filling, but also ultra healthy and super delicious.

MAKES 2 BOWLS

INGREDIENTS

Quinoa Superfood Salad

- 1 cup quinoa, rinsed
- 1/2 teaspoon salt
- 1 capsicum, finely chopped
- 1 avocado, sliced
- 1 spring onion, sliced
- 1 medium beetroot, uncooked
- 1/2 cup pomegranate seeds
- 1 bunch lettuce
- 1/2 cup walnuts, unsalted

Dressing

- 1 teaspoon agave syrup
- 1 tablespoon Dijon mustard
- 1 tablespoon white balsamic vinegar
- Juice of 1 lime
- 1/3 teaspoon salt
- 1/3 teaspoon pepper
- 3 tablespoons olive oil
- 1 clove garlic, chopped
- 1 onion, chopped
- 1 bunch coriander, chopped

METHOD

Quinoa Superfood Salad

1. Rinse quinoa well, then boil water in a saucepan. Add quinoa and salt and turn it down to medium heat. Cover the saucepan and simmer for approx. 20–30 minutes until all the water has evaporated.
2. Make the noodles out of the beetroot by using a spiraliser or cut them into cubes.
3. Put the quinoa, capsicum, pomegranate seeds and the spring onions into a big bowl, toss to combine and then scoop into your Coconut Bowls together with the lettuce and beetroot noodles.
4. Top the quinoa salad with some walnuts and the sliced avocado.

Dressing

5. Mix agave syrup, Dijon mustard, white balsamic vinegar, lime juice, salt, pepper and olive oil until combined.
6. Cook garlic lightly in a frying pan with the olive oil.
7. Add all dressing ingredients together and serve with the quinoa superfood salad.

Carina Koelle @fan_tasty_c
Carina is a passionate veterinarian and vegan foodie from Germany. Carina loves animals and can't imagine living without them. Her other passion is photography, which has led to her becoming a vegan recipe creator and food blogger.

Green Cauliflower Soup

A delicious and healthy soup, packed with nutrition and plenty of flavour that will warm you up on cold winter days. You'll be coming back for more! It is also a great option to cook in bulk and freeze in batches for a quick meal in the future.

MAKES 4 BOWLS

INGREDIENTS

- 1 medium cauliflower, cut into florets
- 3 cloves garlic, minced
- 1 onion, diced
- 4 cups vegetable stock
- 3/4 teaspoon salt
- 1 teaspoon mixed herbs
- 1 cup coconut milk
- 2 tablespoons nutritional yeast
- 2 large handfuls baby spinach (or 3 teaspoons green superfood powder)

METHOD

1. Place the cauliflower on a lined baking tray, cover with foil and bake for 40 mins at 160°C, turning once.
2. In a non-stick frying pan, saute the onion and garlic for two minutes, adding a little water to avoid sticking.
3. Add the stock, salt, herbs and baked cauliflower, and cook on low for 15 minutes.
4. Remove from heat and put in a high-speed blender with coconut milk and blend until smooth.
5. Add the nutritional yeast and spinach or green powder and blend again.
6. Serve in your Coconut Bowls and top with any leftover cauliflower and chickpeas, if desired.

Jo Ross @healthyeating_jo
Jo lives in Sydney and is a mum of two. She's a plant-based food blogger who turned her passion for food and photography into a career, after 20 years in the corporate sector. She loves making healthier versions of her favourite foods, and turning food into art.

Sesame Falafel Bowl with Beet Dressing

If mouth-watering falafel are your thing, then this sesame falafel bowl recipe will be jumping to the top of your favourite recipe list. Easy and versatile, this combo of falafel and beet dressing is equally perfect as a snack or served up in any salad or veggie bowl.

MAKES 2 BOWLS

INGREDIENTS

Falafel (makes 10 balls)
- 230g cooked chickpeas
- 2 spring onions, chopped
- 2 cloves of garlic
- 1/2 cup parsley, chopped
- 1 tablespoon lemon juice
- 2 tablespoons olive oil
- 1 teaspoon ground cumin
- 1 teaspoon smoked paprika
- 3 tablespoons rice or corn flour
- 3 tablespoons sesame seeds
- Sea salt

Beet Dressing:
- 1 cup natural plant based yoghurt
- Juice of 1 small beetroot
- 1 clove garlic
- 1 teaspoon apple cider vinegar
- Sea salt

METHOD

Falafel
1. Pre-heat the oven to 225°C.
2. In a high-speed blender, combine the chickpeas, spring onions, clove garlics, parsley, lemon juice, olive oil, cumin and smoked paprika. Blend all ingredients and season with salt.
3. Add the rice flour, 1 tablespoon at a time and blend until the mixture is no longer wet. Put everything into a bowl and chill in the refrigerator for 30 minutes.
4. Form the mixture into small balls with your hands and coat in sesame seeds. Place them on a baking tray covered with baking paper and bake in the oven for 20–25 minutes, turning halfway through, until golden brown.

Dressing
5. Prepare the beet dressing by mixing all the ingredients in a bowl until smooth.

To Serve
6. Serve the falafel in your Coconut Bowls with your favourite vegetables, drizzled with the beet dressing.

Bahare Torkamani @healthy_belly
Bahare is a Persian-Swedish girl living in Stockholm. She's always been interested in food, food styling and photography, which has led to @healthy_belly, a space where she explores her own creativity and shares the things that she is passionate about. It is a place where Bahare wants to inspire and get inspired, learn and improve, and keep sharing her passion for food and photography.

Red Beet Zoodles with Minty Crumbled 'Feta'

*Red beet hummus is one of my all-time favourite spreads, sauces
and dips. Fanny often makes a whole batch at the beginning of the week
and creates different dishes around it. After trying it with zoodles,
it was instantly a winner and we're not surprised.*

MAKES 2 BOWLS

INGREDIENTS

Beet Hummus Sauce
- 2 beetroot, steamed
- 140g chickpeas, cooked
- 1 teaspoon cumin seeds
- Juice of 1/4 lemon
- 1 tablespoon olive oil
- 1 teaspoon salt
- 100ml water

Mint Tofu 'Feta'
- 150g tofu
- 1 teaspoon fresh or dried mint, chopped
- Juice of 1/4 lemon
- 1 tablespoon olive oil
- 1/2 teaspoon salt

Other Ingredients
- 4 medium zucchinis
- 2 handfuls rocket
- 1 fig cut into wedges
- 2 tablespoons pecans, chopped
- Mint, to garnish

Tahini Dressing
- Juice of 1/4 lemon
- 1 teaspoon salt
- 1 tablespoon tahini
- 1 tablespoon water

METHOD

1. For the tofu 'feta', crumble the tofu into a bowl and add mint, lemon juice, olive oil and salt. Mix and marinate for at least 30 minutes.
2. For the hummus, put all the ingredients into a high-speed blender and blend until smooth.
3. Pour 1 cup hummus into a mixing bowl. Pour the rest into a jar and store in the fridge for up to 4 days.
4. Spiralise the zucchini into zoodles, and add to the hummus and mix until all of the zoodles are covered in hummus.
5. Place a handful of rocket into each of your Coconut Bowls. Top with the red beet zoodles and garnish with figs, tofu 'feta', pecans and fresh mint.
6. Combine all tahini dressing ingredients and drizzle over the top.

Fanny Frey @fannythefoodie
Fanny is a passionate food photographer, recipe creator and blogger from Switzerland. She is passionate about yoga and running, and studies art history and the theeory of photography. Fanny has also created her own cookbook, *Seasons – A Year in Recipes.*

Vegan 'Fish' Tofu Salad

"Are these tofu for sure? Because they taste just like fish. I can't believe it, this is so delicious!" said a friend of mine, when I served her this tofu salad. That should be all the inspiration you need to create this delicious and nutritious tofu salad recipe.

MAKES 3 BOWLS

INGREDIENTS

'Fish' tofu
- 1 block of firm tofu (300–400g)
- 2 tablespoons fish spices (old bay seasoning)
- 1 tablespoon coconut oil
- 2 tablespoons soy sauce
- 1 teaspoon nutritional yeast

Salad
- 3 cups baby rocket
- 1 avocado, sliced
- 1 cup grape tomatoes, cut in half
- 1 watermelon radish, thinly sliced
- 1 cucumber, sliced lengthways and rolled into ribbons
- 9 broccolini, sliced
- 1 tablespoon hemp hearts

Dressing
- Juice of 1 lemon
- 1 teaspoon olive oil
- 1 teaspoon Dijon mustard
- 1 teaspoon of soy sauce
- Pinch of black pepper

METHOD

1. Remove the tofu from its packaging, drain and wrap with a paper towel to remove extra moisture.
2. Cut the tofu block into 7 rectangles, then cut each rectangle diagonally into 2 triangles. You should have 14 triangles in total.
3. Place the tofu slices on a baking sheet and season with fish spices. Sprinkle a teaspoon over each side, making sure all the tofu slices are well coated with the spices.
4. Warm the coconut oil in a large non-stick pan on medium to high. Add the tofu to the hot oil in a single layer and pan fry on each side for 4–5 minutes or until golden brown.
5. Pour soy sauce over the tofu and let sizzle for a minute, then sprinkle nutritional yeast on and let cook for another 4 minutes or until crispy. Transfer the crispy tofu to a plate to cool while you prepare your salad.
6. Assemble your salad in your Coconut Bowls by adding all the salad ingredients on a bed of baby rocket. Top with the 'fish' tofu.
7. Whisk dressing ingredients in a small bowl and drizzle onto salad.

Tip: The tofu should be consumed no longer than an hour after cooking, otherwise it will start losing its crispiness.

Nathalie Sader @nathaliesader
Nathalie Sader is a holistic health coach with a Master in Clinical Psychology. She is a vegan chef on a mission to empower women to love themselves unconditionally through healing their relationship with food and other healthy rituals.

Zoodles with Sweet Potato Flowers & Baked Mushrooms

This delicious zoodles recipe will both satisfy and nourish your body. The sweet potato flowers are simply irresistible with the herb and spice seasoning. You may want to create some extra to snack on later.

MAKES 2-3 BOWLS

INGREDIENTS

- 150g mushrooms, sliced
- 4 tablespoons coconut milk
- Salt and pepper
- 1 large sweet potato, peeled and sliced into circular slices about 1cm thick
- 4 tablespoons extra virgin olive oil
- 1 tablespoon dried herbs
- 1/8 teaspoon ground turmeric
- 1/4 teaspoon ground ginger
- 5 zucchinis
- 1/2 avocado
- 1 cup baby spinach

METHOD

1. Pre-heat the oven to 180°C.
2. Toss the mushrooms in half the coconut milk. Season with salt and pepper, then place on a baking tray lined with baking paper and bake them for about 20 minutes.
3. Take a small cookie cutter and cut out flowers or whatever shape you like.
4. Put sweet potato flowers in a bowl and season them with half the olive oil, half the dried herbs and all the spices. Line a tray with baking paper and bake for approximately 30 minutes, until the flowers are crispy on the outside and soft in the middle.
5. Using a spiraliser, prepare the zoodles.
6. Heat remaining olive oil in a large saucepan, add the zoodles and let them cook for just a couple of minutes, adding a bit of salt.
7. Transfer the zoodles to a plate and, while they cool down, mash the avocado with the remaining coconut milk and a pinch of salt and toss the zoodles in this sauce.
8. Place a bed of spinach on the bottom of your Coconut Bowls and top with the zoodles, baked mushrooms and sweet potatoes.

Ambra Torelli @littlebitesofbeauty
Ambra was born and raised in Italy, in a family of extremely talented cooks. During her adolescent years, she started developing hypothyroidism and leaky gut issues before realising that by adjusting her diet and lifestyle, she could dramatically improve her situation. Ambra now uses her experience and blog to inspire health-conscious and motivated women who are determined to take control of their health in a natural way.

Zucchini Rice Rolls with Beans

*These zucchini rolls are full of delicious flavours and will become
a summer favourite of yours.*

MAKES 6-8 ROLLS

INGREDIENTS

Rice
- 1 red onion, chopped finely
- Peanut oil
- Pinch of cinnamon
- 1 teaspoon ginger powder
- 1 tablespoon turmeric
- 1 1/2 cups sticky cooked rice
- Sea salt and pepper
- Small bunch dill
- Small bunch mint leaves
- 3 ripe tomatoes, chopped finely

Bean Paste
- 250g kidney beans, rinsed
- Basil, chopped
- 1/2 chilli, chopped
- Pinch of garlic, mashed
- Green olives, chopped
- 1 tablespoon lime juice
- 1 shallot, chopped finely

Rolls
- 1–2 large zucchinis, sliced long
  and blanched

METHOD

1. Lightly fry red onion in peanut oil, add cinnamon, ginger powder
   and turmeric. Remove from heat. Add cooked rice and combine
   everything well. Add salt, dill, mint and tomatoes.
2. For the bean paste, mash the beans with a fork and add the rest
   of the bean paste ingredients. Stir.
3. Take a zucchini slice and rice and press down. Take the second
   zucchini slice and cover with the rice. Top with bean paste, lightly
   press and make a roll.
4. Skewer to keep rolls together and serve in your Coconut Bowls.

Kathrin Salzwedel @klaraslife
Katherin is a food blogger and lives in south Germany with her boyfriend, Ramin, where they
both love creating and sharing healthy plant-based food. Their food philosophy is to use fresh
local produce as often as possible.

Green Goodness Noodle Bowl

This is a bowl for your mind, body and soul. Your eyes will sparkle and your mouth will water; this nutritious green goodness noodle bowl truly tastes as good as it looks.

MAKES 2 BOWLS

INGREDIENTS

- 1 purple sweet potato or regular sweet potato
- 2 portions rice noodles
- Salt
- 1/4 Romanesco broccoli
- 250g edamame
- 1 lemon, sliced
- 6 black olives, sliced
- Parsley, chopped
- 1 avocado, sliced
- 2 tablespoons nutritional yeast
- Pinch of pepper
- 100ml oatmilk
- 1 teaspoon apple cider vinegar

METHOD

1. Bake the sweet potato at 250°C for 20 minutes.
2. Cook the rice noodles in water with a pinch of salt for 2 minutes or according to the instructions. Cook the Romanesco broccoli for 3 minutes and the edamame for 5 minutes.
3. Peel the sweet potato and the edamame, and the lemon, olives, parsley and avocado as you desire.
4. For the sauce, blend the sweet potato with nutritional yeast, a pinch of salt and pepper, oat milk and apple cider vinegar until smooth.
5. Pour sauce over the cooked rice noodles and serve in your Coconut Bowls. Top with the Romanesco broccoli, edamame, lemon, olives, avocado and parsley.

Jeanette Vaß en @vegansoulfoody
Netti lives in Germany and has both Serbian and German roots. She has always lived close to animals and, from an early age, learnt to respect them and live in harmony with Mother Nature. Netti lives a healthy, vegan lifestyle and loves cooking with natural ingredients. She has studied animal psychology and has been active in animal rescue for more than 15 years.

Super Simple Zoodle Salad with Lime Peanut Sauce

A light, nutritious salad to satisfy everyone's belly. This salad has many reasons to be loved and it is super fuss free. The sauce in this dish can also be used for dipping salad rolls, pouring on rice or in stir fries.

MAKES 4 BOWLS

INGREDIENTS

Zoodle Salad
- 3 medium zucchini, spiralised
- 2 medium sized carrots, grated
- 2 cups red cabbage, thinly sliced and roughly chopped
- 1/2 cup coriander, chopped
- 1/4 cup spring onion, thinly sliced
- 4 tablespoons sunflower seeds

Dressing
- 3 tablespoons olive oil
- Juice of 1 lime
- 1 tablespoon hot sauce
- 1 heaped tablespoon peanut butter
- Pinch of pink Himalayan sea salt
- Pinch of fresh cracked black pepper
- 1 tablespoon black sesame seeds
- Water, for a runnier consistency

Toppings
- Lime wedges
- Crushed peanuts (optional)

METHOD

1. To make the dressing, add all the dressing ingredients to a mason jar, seal the lid and shake well. If you add water to create a runnier consistency, just make sure you are adding a little at a time (a tablespoon or so). Set aside.
2. Put all the vegetables into a large mixing bowl and stir gently using your hands.
3. Serve in your Coconut Bowls and garnish with sesame seeds, a generous serving of the dressing and lime wedges.

Tip: This salad lasts in the fridge for up to 2 days, but make sure you keep the dressing separate to avoid a soggy salad.

Maria Koutsogiannis @foodbymaria
Maria is a healthy, Greek-Canadian fitness and food enthusiast. She is the food stylist, recipe creator, photographer and writer behind the foodbymaria.com blog. Maria is a lover of organic whole foods, all things green and plant-based eating.

Unicorn Noodles

*A quick and easy way to impress kids and adults alike. Nobody will guess
that it is all natural and requires just three ingredients!*

INGREDIENTS

Noodles
- 3 cups red cabbage, roughly chopped
- 1.5L water
- 2 serves clear or white noodles
- Juice of 1 lemon

Toppings:
- Avocado
- Micro greens
- Your favourite vegan sauce

METHOD

1. Place the cabbage and water in a saucepan and simmer on a medium heat until the water is a deep purple colour. Make sure not to rapidly boil the cabbage, or it will turn brown.
2. Once water is purple (approx. 5–10 mins), remove the cabbage from the pot and place noodles in the purple water.
3. Cook noodles on medium heat for the amount of time specified on the packet.
4. Once cooked, strain the noodles and place in a large bowl. The noodles should be a blueish colour at this stage.
5. Add lemon juice to the areas you want to be pink. For purple, add a small amount of lemon juice and mix around. The more lemon juice you add, the pinker the noodles will get.
6. Divide between two Coconut Bowls and add your favourite sauce and toppings. I use avocado and microgreens to keep things simple, but your meal is only limited by your imagination.

Ami Shoesmith @the_sunkissed_kitchen
Ami is a Sydney-based vegan food stylist from Australia. She has a passion for sharing healthy food with others and inspiring people to eat the rainbow.

Citrus Soba Noodle Salad

A sweet, zesty and hearty salad perfect for any occasion. The sweetness combined with the tanginess work well together to create an Asian-inspired dish that truly satisfies.

MAKES 2 BOWLS

INGREDIENTS

Salad
- 1/2 packet soba noodles
- 1 head broccoli, cut into pieces
- 1 large carrot, peeled and cut into matchsticks
- 2 cucumbers, cut into matchsticks
- 1 tablespoon sesame seeds

Dressing
- 1/4 teaspoon cayenne pepper
- 1 clove garlic
- 1 teaspoon finely grated ginger
- Juice of 1/2 lime
- 2 teaspoon maple syrup
- Juice of 1/2 orange
- 2 tablespoons soy sauce
- 2 tablespoons sesame oil
- 2 tablespoons extra virgin olive oil

METHOD

1. Add soba noodles to a pot of salted boiling water, allow to cook for 4-6 minutes. Drain and rinse under cold water. Set aside.
2. Blanch broccoli for 1 minute. Rinse under cold water immediately. Set aside.
3. Add the soba noodles, carrots, cucumber and broccoli to a large bowl or pot.
4. Prepare the dressing by adding all the ingredients to a bowl and stirring. Pour the dressing over the noodles and mix through.
5. Serve in your Coconut Bowls and top with a sprinkle of sesame seeds. Best served cold.

Melissa D'Elia @the_vibrantvegan
Melissa is from Melbourne, Australia, and studies nutritional science. She is passionate about veganism/plant-based diets and sustainability, and aspires to educate and encourage others to live a vegan lifestyle. Melissa also loves food photography/filmography and fashion.

Mango Summer Rolls with Peanut Sauce

Fresh summer rolls are the perfect picnic snack under the warm sunshine! Enjoy the bursting flavours of the mango and coriander dipped in the sweet peanut sauce.

MAKES 8-10 ROLLS

INGREDIENTS

Rolls

- 1 medium cucumber
- 1 mango
- 8–10 rice paper sheets
- 2 cups sprouts
- 1/2 cup coriander leaves

- ### Sauce
- 1 cup peanut butter
- 1/4 cup coconut sugar
- 1/4 cup water

METHOD

Rolls

1. Thinly slice the cucumber, mango, and cabbage.
2. Unwrap the rice paper sheets and place one sheet in 5 cm of water. Soak for 20–30 seconds.
3. Take the rice paper out of the water and lay on a flat surface.
4. Layer the ingredients. Add a large pinch of sprouts to the centre of the rice paper. Layer on top with coriander, cabbage, mango, and cucumber.
5. Fold the rice paper like a burrito. Take the far side of the sheet and fold it over the ingredients. Take the bottom and top sides and fold them over tightly. Continue to roll like a burrito until it is tight and connected.
6. Enjoy a large summer roll or cut them in half for serving in your Coconut Bowls.

Sauce

7. In a small bowl, add the peanut butter, coconut sugar and water.
8. Stir until the water and sugar have absorbed into the peanut butter.
9. Serve alongside the rolls for dipping.

Kiely Graves @thekindcoconut
Kiely, from The Kind Coconut, is a health and lifestyle blogger from California. A vegan since she was 17, Kiely is passionate about health, fitness and helping others. As any good Californian will tell you, they're at home on a beach under the warm sun.

Rainbow 'Leftovers' Buddha Bowl

The ultimate buddha bowl or, as I like to call it, the 'leftovers bowl'. Packed to the brim with nutritious vegetables that will empty your fridge and fill your body with goodness. All ingredients can be substituted.

MAKES 2 BOWLS

INGREDIENTS

- 1 zucchini, cut into strips
- 1 cup broccoli, chopped
- 1/2 cup peas
- 1/2 cup corn
- 1/2 cup red cabbage, sliced
- 1/2 cup micro greens
- 1/2 avocado, chopped
- 1/2 tomato, cut into wedges
- 1 cup lettuce
- 2 tablespoons vegan pesto (see recipe page 256)
- 2 tablespoons pomegranate seeds

METHOD

1. Grill the zucchini in coconut oil in a hot pan.
2. Steam the broccoli.
3. To arrange the bowl, first wash the lettuce and create a lettuce bed in the bottom of your Coconut Bowls.
4. Next, place the zucchini, peas, broccoli, tomatoes, avocado, corn, red and red cabbage in sections around the bowl.
5. Sprinkle over the micro greens, pomegranate seeds and dress in pesto.

Tip: Add shaved or slivered almonds for extra texture.

Tasha Meys @tastefullytash
Tasha is a Kiwi health-food nut living in LA. She's passionate about all things health, wellness, art, photography and food. Tasha loves to create healthy and delicious recipes for others to enjoy and use. Her goal is to help people see how rewarding it is when you nourish your body from the inside out.

Ultimate Comfort Macaroni

A comfort food classic. Perfect for families and a great way to use up vegetables. A creamy tomato sauce with aromatic garlic, onion and capsicum with a burst of freshness from the green peas. It is a dish that you can't resist. Add a side of olives and some delicious toasted bread for extra body, and it is a perfect small meal.

MAKES 4–5 BOWLS

INGREDIENTS

Macaroni

- 500g macaroni
- 1 tablespoon olive oil
- 1 onion, diced
- 2 cloves garlic, minced
- 1 red capsicum, diced
- 400g frozen peas
- 3 packed cups spinach (or any other veggie)
- 700g tomato basil pasta sauce (or any tomato-based sauce from your local grocery store)
- Salt and black pepper
- Nutritional yeast (optional)

Sides

- Olives
- Toasted bread

METHOD

1. Fill a pot with water and add a tablespoon of salt and allow it to come to a boil. Once boiling, add the macaroni and cook for 9 minutes. Stir occasionally so that the macaroni doesn't stick to each other or the bottom of the pot.
2. In the meantime, add olive oil to a pan on high heat and add the diced onion. Cook until translucent. Then add the garlic and allow to cook with the onion for 30 seconds. Then add the capsicum and allow to cook lightly for 2 minutes before adding the frozen peas. Place lid on top of pan and allow the peas to cook for a further 3–4 minutes. Add the tomato basil pasta sauce then turn the heat off the pan.
3. At this point, the macaroni should be cooked. Don't drain all of the pasta water, scoop water out cup by cup until all off the macaroni is visible.
4. Add the sauce from the pan to the pasta and stir evenly.
5. Taste test time. Add salt and pepper to taste.
6. Turn off the heat from under the pasta, add the spinach on top and cover the pot to allow the spinach to wilt before stirring into the pasta.
7. Scoop into Coconut Bowls and garnish with nutritional yeast if desired. Serve with sides of olives and toasted bread.

Amina Maswadeh @arabfruitlady
Amina is an American Muslim woman who is extremely passionate about health and nutrition. Amina's journey and passion started from the struggles of trying to find her identity and battling with society's expectations. This resulted in developing bad relationships with herself, her body, and food. Amina knows that others go through similar experiences and wants to offer people a helping hand if they need one. Her goal is to create, have fun and, most importantly, spread love.

Vegan Tortellini with Guacamole & Peas

Tortellini and guacamole? It takes confidence and talent to pair these two favourites, and I have delivered this in a recipe that will connect your smile and taste buds like nothing before. Served chilled, and enjoy!

MAKES 2 BOWLS

INGREDIENTS

- 2 avocados
- 1 red onion, finely chopped
- 2 cloves garlic, crushed
- Juice of 1 lime
- Salt and pepper
- 250g vegan tortellini
- 1/2 cup peas

METHOD

1. Mash avocados in a bowl.
2. Stir in onion and garlic.
3. Add lime juice and salt and pepper to taste.
4. Chill for half an hour to blend the flavours.
5. In the meantime, cook peas and tortellini in the same or separate pots, according to instructions on the packages.
6. Drain and rinse with cold water and chill for 30 minutes.
7. Combine tortellini with guacamole and peas in your Coconut Bowl.

Bianca Zapatka @biancazapatka
Bianca is a German fitness and nutrition coach who loves to create colourful, delicious and healthy recipes. You'll be inspired by all the beautiful food photos and recipes on Bianca's blog and Instagram page.

Colourful Confetti Chickpea Salad with Sliced Avocado

This rainbow confetti salad is a nutritional powerhouse. Packed with plant proteins, healthy fats, vitamins and antioxidants, this salad is a treat for your taste buds without the need for any sauce or dressing.

MAKES 3-4 BOWLS

Salad
- 1 1/2 cups green beans, chopped
- 1 stalk celery, diced
- 1/2 small cucumber, diced
- 5-6 radishes, diced
- 1/4 cup red onion, diced
- 1 small yellow capsicum, diced
- 400g chickpeas
- 11/2 avocados, sliced
- 1/4 cup dill or other fresh herbs

Dressing
- 1/4 cup olive oil or flax oil
- 1/4 apple cider vinegar
- 1 teaspoon Dijon mustard
- 1/2 teaspoon salt
- 1/2 teaspoon maple syrup

METHOD

1. Steam the green beans until tender.
2. Rinse and drain the chickpeas, and combine in a big bowl with all the veggies.
3. Whisk together the dressing ingredients, and add the desired amount to your salad and serve in your Coconut Bowls.
4. Place on top of the salad. Add some freshly ground pepper, and garnish with the dill.

Anna Pelzer @anna.pelzer
Anna is a vegan food enthusiast and photographer from Vancouver, Canada. She loves combining the creativity of food styling with the technical aspects of photography to show people the many delights of delicious vegan food.

Simple Sushi Bowl

*These simple and easy sushi bowls are nutrient rich and delicious.
One of the best things about this dish is that you can add your own
veggies to match your desired flavour palate.*

MAKES 2-3 BOWLS

INGREDIENTS

- 1 sheet nori
- 1 cup sushi rice, cooked
- 2 small cucumbers, julienned
- Sesame seeds
- 3 carrots, julienned
- 2-3 cups of your favourite greens
- 1/4 cup red onions, sliced
- Sprouts
- Soy sauce

METHOD

1. Lay down the nori sheet on a bamboo mat and spread the rice, leaving about an inch on the top.
2. Next, add half of the cucumbers and sesame seeds down the centre (on the bottom part).
3. Carefully lift the end of the mat and roll it over the ingredients. Lightly press with your hands to ensure that it is a complete roll.
4. Slice the roll into about 8 pieces with a sharp knife.
5. Prepare your Coconut Bowls by adding equal amounts of carrots, greens, onion, sushi slices and leftover cucumbers.
6. Drizzle with soy sauce and sprinkle with extra sesame seeds.

Jasmine Yildiz @earthyjasmine
Jasmine is a health, wellness and lifestyle lover from America. For Jasmine,
nourishing our bodies with wholesome, plant-based foods is the key to a healthy lifestyle.

Chilled Lime, Pea & Spinach Soup

Combining peas and spinach in a soup is both refreshing and nutritious. The spinach tempers the slightly sweet flavour of the peas, keeping it green and savoury. The herbs give it depth while the lime brightens everything. This soup is perfect for both hot and cold weather.

MAKES 4 BOWLS

INGREDIENTS

- 1 handful cashews, soaked in hot water
- 2 cups frozen peas
- 5 spring onions, chopped
- 2 mint leaves, chopped
- 1 teaspoon fresh thyme leaves, chopped
- 1 clove garlic, chopped
- 1 cup spinach
- 1/2 cup water
- Juice of 2 limes
- Pepper and salt

METHOD

1. Thaw the peas for 30 minutes.
2. Put all ingredients in a high-speed blender and blend until smooth.
3. Serve chilled in your Coconut Bowls with a swirl of plant-based yoghurt.

Debbie Dine @greensmoothiegourmet
Debbie (Dee) is a creative, healthy foodie with a passion for plant-based foods, smoothies and symmetry. Greensmoothiegourmet.com is where Debbie shares plant-based recipes that are nutritious, easy to prepare, and typically require only single-digit familiar ingredients.

Asian-Inspired Buddha Bowl

A wholesome and colourful bowl with the best of all worlds, combining lightly sweet tofu with hummus, a light slaw and quinoa.

MAKES 2 BOWLS

INGREDIENTS

- 200g firm tofu, cut into cubes
- 1/4 cup coconut aminos teriyaki sauce (or another teriyaki sauce)
- 1 1/2 cups water
- 1/2 cup quinoa
- 1 cup cooked chickpeas
- Juice of 1 lemon
- Zest of 1 lemon
- 1 tablespoon miso paste
- 1/2 cup carrot, grated
- 1/2 cup red cabbage, shredded
- 1/4 cup edamame beans
- Sesame seeds, to garnish

METHOD

1. Place tofu in a shallow dish. Cover with teriyaki sauce, then set aside.
2. Add water and quinoa to a small saucepan and bring to the boil. Boil for 5 minutes, then reduce to a medium heat, simmering for 15 minutes until the quinoa is cooked. Drain, then set aside.
3. In a high-speed blender, blitz chickpeas with the lemon and miso until a smooth paste is formed.
4. Make the slaw by mixing together the carrot, cabbage and edamame beans in a small bowl.
5. Assemble all ingredients in your Coconut Bowls as desired. Sprinkle with sesame seeds, then serve.

Anthea Cheng @rainbownourishments
Anthea is the chef, food blogger and food stylist behind Rainbow Nourishments. She created Rainbow Nourishments as a way to share colourful and nourishing vegan food with people internationally and in her local community. Anthea uses plant-based ingredients in the hope of creating a more sustainable world and minimising cruelty to animals. She also owns a raw vegan cake business in Canberra, where she creates bespoke cakes for customers and cafes.

Red Lentil Curry Soup

*Curry, soup or broth? You're in charge here. This tasty, red lentil dish
is as versatile as they come. Equally enjoyable with your family, a group
of friends, a special someone or as a leftover lunch.*

MAKES 6 BOWLS

INGREDIENTS

- 3 medium carrots, cubed
- 4 medium potatoes, cubed
- 220g red lentils
- 1 cup grilled corn
- 4 celery stalks, finely chopped
- 1 tablespoon garlic powder
- 1 tablespoon onion powder
- 1 tablespoon curry powder
- 1 teaspoon dried parsley
- Water
- 2 tablespoons veggie stock
  powder, or to taste
- 4 cups kale, chopped
- Salt and pepper

METHOD

1. Put all ingredients (except for kale and stock powder) to a large pot.
2. Add desired amount of water. More water means more broth.
   Use less water for a thicker soup.
3. Cover and cook on high for 5 hours.
4. Take some of the broth and add it to a bowl with your veggie stock
   powder. Mix until the stock powder dissolves and pour into your soup.
   Cover and cook for one more hour.
5. When the soup is cooked, add in kale and stir until well combined.
6. Season with salt and pepper to taste.
7. Serve in your Coconut Bowls with rice or on its own.

Stephanie Williams @veganwhat
Stephanie is a born and raised Californian vegan foodie who loves to bring creative ideas
to life. She is also the founder of Vegan What Apparel, creating fun vegan-themed shirts
and products that spread awareness about veganism. Go Stephanie!

Asian Rice Noodle Soup with Mixed Veggies

The perfect weekday lunch or dinner. Simple, easy, yet delicious and satisfying. This Asian noodle soup is packed with flavour. The only thing to watch out for is the craving for another bowl that may follow.

MAKES 3 BOWLS

INGREDIENTS

- 120g rice noodles
- 500ml vegetable stock
- 1 cup bean sprouts
- 1 chilli, thinly sliced
- 3 chestnuts, cooked and sliced
- 1/2 cup coriander
- 2–3 cloves garlic, grated
- 5–6 slices lotus roots, thinly sliced (can easily be found in Asian supermarkets)
- 1/2 cup mint leaves
- 3 shiitake mushrooms, thinly sliced
- 1/2 cup spring onions, chopped
- 1/2 cup Thai basil
- 5 tablespoons vegetable oil

METHOD

1. Cook noodles according to instructions. Set aside to cool.
2. Bring the vegetable stock to the boil and keep it hot until needed.
3. Heat a frying pan over medium–high heat. When the pan is hot, add the vegetable oil, then add the lotus root slices. Fry both sides until slightly brown and crispy. Take them out and place them on a paper towel-lined plate to drain the excess oil.
4. Using the same frying pan, add garlic and saute for about 2–3 mins or until fragrant. Add shiitake mushrooms and brown them on both sides. Drain on the same paper towel-lined plate as the lotus roots.
5. Divide the cooked noodles among three Coconut Bowls. Then add enough hot vegetable stock so that it just covers the noodles. Then add the bean sprouts, Thai basil, coriander, mint, spring onions, chestnut slices, shiitake mushrooms, chilli and lotus root slices.
6. Serve hot.

Madeline Lu @lumadeline
Madeline loves cooking dishes that are simple, quick, healthy and, most importantly, delicious. Originally from China, she has lived in Europe (UK, Switzerland and Germany) for 15 years. She now resides in San Francisco Bay, California, with her husband and two kids. She draws a lot of food inspiration from her travels and experiences from living in different places.

Rainbow Salad Bowl with Satay Sauce

This vibrant salad is the perfect way to 'eat the rainbow'. Full of crunchy raw veggies, sweet pineapple and topped with a creamy, spicy satay sauce and crunchy peanuts, it makes the perfect light lunch.

MAKES 3 BOWLS

INGREDIENTS

Satay Sauce
- See recipe page 257

Rainbow Salad
- 1 small carrot, peeled into ribbons
- 1 Lebanese cucumber, deseeded and thinly sliced
- 1/2 yellow capsicum, thinly sliced
- 1/2 red capsicum, thinly sliced
- 1/4 small red cabbage, shredded
- 1/2 small pineapple, diced
- 1 bunch Thai basil
- Handful coriander leaves

To Serve
- 1/2 cup crushed dry-roasted peanuts

METHOD

1. Combine all the salad ingredients together in your Coconut Bowls.
2. Top salad with sauce, garnish with crushed peanuts and serve.

Tina Khoury @thebarefoothousewife

Tina is a graphic designer, food stylist, food photographer, wife and mother of three young boys from Sydney, Australia. Tina's approach to food is pretty simple – eat more plants and enjoy them surrounded by friends and family. She loves to know the food she makes will nourish a loved one's body and soul, and that makes her happy. This is a feeling she hopes to pass on to you by sharing recipes on her blog, The Barefoot Housewife.

Mains

CURRIES - PASTAS - MEXICAN

Mains

This is where jaws drop and minds are blown, as talented recipe developers show you their take on global cuisine. Innovation replaces tradition as incredible flavours from all over the world are infused into healthy wholesome classics. We're literally flipping burgers on their head here, with scrumptious smoky beet and sweet potato patties.

Opt for a Mexican feast fit for royalty with taco bowls topped with creamy guacamole and mango salsa. Veggie-based Indian dishes are also hot for the taking, with a number of spicy curries that will put a fire in your belly.

Of course, it wouldn't be a culinary trip around the world without some mention of Italian cuisine. While Nonna might be shaking her head, we promise you won't be, with delicious pillows of potato gnocchi, spinach pasta and unicorn ravioli stuffed with delicious pesto.

Whatever the occasion, there will never be a dull moment when it comes to cooking these satisfying, nourishing and irresistible main meals. Delightful for one, perfect for two, or simply delicious for entertaining the whole family.

Step outside the box and let a world of opportunities take over.
The kitchen's your stage and we're giving you permission to shine.

The Coolest Chilli 'Buddha Bowl'

Chilli. It is a classic comfort food. This one is a twist on your typical version, made of only fruits and vegetables. It is the freshest, coolest chilli you'll ever taste. Filling enough to make it the main dish, or saddle it up as a side to your favourite salad or Buddha bowl ingredients.

MAKES 2 BOWLS

INGREDIENTS

The Tomato Base
- 1/2 teaspoon chilli powder
- 1/2 teaspoon cumin powder
- 4 cloves garlic
- 1 lemon, juiced
- 1/2 brown onion
- 1/8 teaspoon black pepper
- 3 tablespoons raisins
- 2 1/2 cups cherry tomatoes
- 1 1/2 cups sun dried tomatoes

The Veggies
- 1/2 cup capsicum, thinly sliced
- 1 carrot, julienned
- 2 cups celery, thinly chopped
- 6 mushrooms, diced
- 1/4 red onion, thinly sliced
- 1/2 cup cherry tomato, diced
- 1 zucchini, peeled and diced

To Serve
- 2 spring onion stalks, chopped
- 1/4 jalapeño, thinly sliced
- 1/2 cup coriander, chopped

METHOD

1. Place the tomato base ingredients in blender and blend until smooth.
2. Divide the veggie ingredients between your Coconut Bowls.
3. Pour the tomato base over veggies and thoroughly mix together.
4. Garnish with spring onion, jalapeño and coriander. If you're brave, and like it extra spicy, add a little more jalapeño.

Mel Pampanin @absofruitlymel
Mel is an LA-native, fruit-loving vegan living in Santa Monica, California. She works at MUSE School by day and spends her spare time running on the beach and creating in the kitchen. Mel's wish is for everyone to experience the fruitful benefits of healthy eating, and her mission is to make it easy, delicious, and enjoyable for people to include more fruit and vegetables on their plate and in their lives.

Taco Bowl with Mango Salsa

This summer taco recipe is a real crowd pleaser. The mango salsa gives your tastebuds a fresh, sweet and summery flavour, and the creamy guacamole is a must. Veggies give it the perfect crunch, while the protein packed lentil and quinoa base is so delicious mixed with the taco spices.

MAKES 4 BOWLS

INGREDIENTS

Tacos
- 1 cup green lentils, cooked
- 2 cups quinoa, cooked
- 1 red capsicum, diced
- 1/3 cucumber, diced
- 150g cherry tomatoes, diced
- 8 lettuce leaves, sliced

Mango Salsa
- 1 mango, sliced into small cubes
- 1/4 red onion, diced
- 2 tablespoons coriander, diced
- 1/2 red chilli pepper, diced
- Juice of 1/2 lime

Guacamole
- See recipe page 257

Taco Spice Mix
- 1 teaspoon chilli flakes
- 4 teaspoons cumin
- 2 teaspoons garlic powder
- 2 teaspoons ground coriander
- 3 teaspoons paprika powder
- 1/2 teaspoon salt

METHOD

1. Mix together the lentils, quinoa and the taco spice.
2. To make the mango salsa, put mango, onion, coriander leaves and red chilli in a bowl. Add the lime juice and mix all of the ingredients together.
3. Divide the taco ingredients, lettuce, salsa and guacamole in your Coconut Bowls.

Tip: A pre-made taco spice mix pack can also be purchased from your local store. In this case, use 4 heaped tablespoons.

Siri Harsem @awildflowerlife
Siri is a recipe creator, YouTuber and lover of healthy and delicious food from Norway. Siri loves trying out new recipes, experimenting in the kitchen and sharing her creations with others to hopefully inspire them to live healthier.

Chickpea Zucchini Eggplant Potato Curry

This is an easy and warming curry recipe, that is great to have on those chilly nights. You can change the vegetables to use what's in season (always tastier and better for the planet!) and pair with your choice of grain (all rice, quinoa, millet, bulgur, etc... all go so well with it).

MAKES 4 BOWLS

INGREDIENTS

- 2 small potatoes, cut into cubes
- 1/2 cup brown grain rice
- 2 tablespoons coconut oil
- 2 cloves garlic, minced
- 1 small brown onion, chopped
- 1/2 medium zucchini, chopped
- 1 small eggplant, chopped
- 200g cooked chickpeas, chopped
- Pinch of salt
- 2 tablespoons tomato paste
- 1 tablespoon curry powder
- 250ml coconut milk

METHOD

1. Start by boiling the potatoes and rice for 20 minutes while you prepare the rest of ingredients.
2. In a pan, heat coconut oil and when it is warm enough, add garlic and onion. Saute both for 2 minutes.
3. Now add zucchini and eggplant and saute for about 10–15 minutes, until all vegetables are soft.
4. Add boiled potatoes and chickpeas to the pan and stir to combine.
5. Add salt to taste, tomato paste and curry powder to the pan and stir again to combine.
6. Pour coconut milk on top and stir yet again, to make sure all ingredients are properly mixed.
7. Let mixture simmer on low-medium heat for 10–15 minutes (this depends on how thick you'd like the sauce to be).
8. Serve in the Coconut Bowls and add fresh garnish (parsley is my favourite).

Consuelo Morcillo @earthlytaste
Consuela is a Spanish food photographer by day and a professional puppy petter by night, who enjoys eating all plants, riding her bike outdoors and dancing away the night at music festivals.

Mexican Lentil Chilli Bowl

This recipe is a staple in my house – I make it about once a week (and leftovers last for a couple of extra meals as well). Enjoy as Mexican chilli bowls when made fresh; and for leftovers, treat yourself to an awesome burrito.

MAKES 4 BOWLS

INGREDIENTS

- 1 cup brown rice
- 1 onion, diced finely
- 1 capsicum, diced finely
- 1 carrot, diced finely
- 3 medium tomatoes, diced
- 1 tablespoon mustard
- 1 tablespoon Cajun spice mix
- 300–400g (can) refried beans
- 300–400g (can) lentils, rinsed well and drained
- 1 cob fresh corn, cooked, then slice the corn from the cob (or use canned)

To Serve
- Avocado
- Coriander
- Tortillas
- Green salad

METHOD

1. Pop your brown rice on to cook.
2. Heat a small amount of water in a large non-stick pan over a medium heat. Add in onion and saute for a few minutes.
3. Add in capsicum, carrot, tomatoes, mustard and Cajun spice mix, and stir for about 5 minutes.
4. Add in the rest of the ingredients (beans, lentils and corn) and mix well.
5. Continue to cook and stir for about 10 minutes, or until it reaches the desired consistency and all the veggies are cooked.
6. Serve up in your Coconut Bowls.

Andrea Brown @eatwithandy
Andy is an Australian recipe creator and blogger. A lover of sunshine, yoga and plant based eats, her love affair with vegan food began after years of suffering with an autoimmune disease, IBS symptoms and an unhealthy approach to eating.

Spicy Coconut Pumpkin Curry

This spicy curry is a delicious warming dish that will be a new favourite amongst your family. It is super easy to make and sure to satisfy.

MAKES 2 BOWLS

INGREDIENTS

- 1 brown onion, chopped
- 5 tablespoons curry powder
- 3 tablespoons paprika powder
- 1 small pumpkin, cubed
- 3 potatoes, cubed
- 100g cherry tomatoes, cut into small pieces
- 100g green beans
- 400ml coconut milk
- 600ml vegetable stock
- Basmati rice, to serve

METHOD

1. Put the onion into a pan with the spices and a little water for about 4 minutes on medium-low heat.
2. Add your veggies and then, after 6 minutes, add the coconut milk and your vegetable stock.
3. Boil your desired amount of basmati rice in a separate pot.
4. Let the curry cook for about 25 minutes, stirring occasionally for a creamy consistency, feel free to add salt and pepper to taste.
5. Place a bed of basmati rice in your Coconut Bowls, scoop on the curry and serve.

Anna Peemöller @goodfood_annaslife
Anna is a teenage vegan food blogger from Hamburg, Germany. She loves to create plant-based recipes for her little community and to show that you can make your dreams comes true, you just need to believe in yourself!

Falafel Balls with Spinach Pasta

Leila's falafels are so, so good – so don't be surprised if you need to pick your tongue up off the ground. Served with spinach noodles, this delicious dish will leave you craving more. The recipe feeds two, but keep that second bowl for yourself if you really can't resist.

MAKES 2 BOWLS

INGREDIENTS

Falafel
- 400g chickpeas, boiled
- 2 tablespoons ground flax seeds
- 1/2 onion, diced
- 3 cloves garlic, mashed
- 3 tablespoons flour
- 1/2 teaspoon paprika
  or dried chilli flakes
- 1 cup fresh parsley, chopped
- 1/2 teaspoon salt
- 1/2 teaspoon black pepper
- 1/2 teaspoon ground cumin
- 1 tablespoon tahini paste

Pasta & Sauce
- 200g spinach noodles
  (or zoodles)
- 1/2 onion, minced
- 100ml coconut milk
- 1 teaspoon salt
- 1/2 teaspoon black pepper
- 3 teaspoons curry powder
- 1 teaspoon tahini paste

METHOD

Falafel
1. Blend all ingredients in a high-speed blender.
2. Heat some oil in a non-stick frying pan.
3. Make the patties (1 heaped tablespoon per patty) and fry for 2 minutes.
4. Put the falafels on a plate covered with paper towel (to absorb all excess oil).

Pasta & Sauce
5. Add water in a pot, add salt to taste and bring the water to a boil. Add the noodles.
6. Heat some oil in a non-stick frying pan.
7. Fry the onions for 4 minutes, then add the coconut milk and all your spices.
8. Cook for 5 minutes, stirring occasionally to achieve a creamy texture.
9. Add the pasta to your Coconut Bowls, then top with the falafels and drizzle on the sauce.

Leila Jasmin @leilajasmin_
Leila is a German blogger promoting body positivity and self-confidence. She loves to cook fresh and healthy food and share it with her friends, family and social media community.

Unicorn Ravioli with Hemp Pesto

Prepare for this easy unicorn ravioli to become your new favourite pasta dish. It is hard to believe that this completely edible piece of art is made from all-natural ingredients. Create, admire and enjoy!

MAKES 2 BOWLS

INGREDIENTS

Ravioli
- 3 cups wholewheat flour
- 1 teaspoon salt
- 40ml beetroot juice
- 40ml spinach juice
- 40ml water
- Tomatoes, chopped, to serve
- Fresh basil, chopped, to serve

Hemp Pesto
- 1 1/2 cups hemp
- 1/2 cup spinach
- 1/2 cup basil
- 1/2 cup cashews
- 100ml olive oil
- 1 teaspoon salt
- 1 teaspoon black pepper
- Lemon juice

METHOD

1. Divide the flour between 3 bowls.
2. Add a pinch of salt to each bowl. Then add beetroot juice to one, spinach juice to the other and water in the third bowl.
3. Knead on a floured surface with your hands.
4. Mix the 3 doughs together and thinly roll them out.
5. Meanwhile add all the ingredients for the pesto to a high-speed blender. Then cut the dough into round circles and fill each one with a teaspoon of pesto, pressing the edges together once filled (you can use a tool for this).
6. Bring a pot of water to the boil. Add salt and the ravioli, and cook for 2–5 minutes.
7. Serve with fresh tomatoes and fresh basil in your Coconut Bowls.

Lena Pfetzer @lenaliciously
Lena is crazy about tasty and healthy vegan food. She began blogging after receiving so much support for her fruit platters. She strives to inspire people with her little edible pieces of art and homemade vegan recipes.

Mustard & Curry Leaf Rice

This is a very popular recipe. While curry leaves add a special flavour to the dish, there is more to the humble curry leaf than just taste – they're packed with carbohydrates, fibre, calcium, iron and many other added benefits.

MAKES 4 BOWLS

INGREDIENTS

- 1 tablespoon coconut oil
- 6 curry leaves
- 1 teaspoon mustard seeds
- 1 medium onion, finely chopped
- 1 teaspoon garam masala
- 2 tablespoons shredded coconut
- 1 cup vegetables of your choice, coarsely chopped (carrot, purple cabbage, green cabbage, etc.)
- 1 tablespoon lemon juice
- 1 teaspoon coconut sugar
- 1 teaspoon turmeric powder
- 1 cup steamed rice
- 1/4 cup cashews, to garnish
- 1/4 cup raisins, to garnish
- Cherry tomatoes, halved (optional)
- Salt

METHOD

1. Heat oil in a large non-stick pan over medium heat. Add curry leaves and mustard seeds. Once the seeds start to crackle, add onion and fry until golden.
2. Add garam masala, shredded coconut and cook for a further 2 minutes. Season with salt. Add vegetables and cook for another 2 minutes. Stir through the lemon, coconut sugar, turmeric and steamed rice until combined.
3. Serve in your Coconut Bowls and top with cashews, raisins and tomatoes.

Monisha Singh @monsflavors
Monisha is a passionate cook and recipe developer who grew up in India and now resides in New Zealand with her husband and two kids. Mon loves to bring happiness to people through real food. Arrive at Mon's house on short notice, and she'll serve up an amazing and delicious meal for everyone.

Mint Basil Pesto Pasta

This mint basil pesto is the perfect summertime pasta. Fresh basil offers a punch of flavour while mint provides a refreshing kick. Try sourcing different varieties of basil and mint from your local farmers' market – they'll have the good stuff. Toasted almonds, nutritional yeast and miso give the pesto a cheesiness that will leave you craving for more and more.

MAKES 4-6 BOWLS

INGREDIENTS

- 2 cups packed basil, plus extra to garnish
- 2 cups packed mint, plus extra to garnish
- 1/2 cup packed chives
- 1/4 cup water
- 1 teaspoon mellow white or chickpea miso
- 3 small cloves garlic, roughly chopped
- 1 teaspoon lemon zest
- 2-3 tablespoons lemon juice
- 1/2 teaspoon sugar or agave nectar
- 1/2 teaspoon freshly cracked pepper, plus extra to taste
- 1/2 teaspoon sea salt, plus extra to taste
- 1/4 teaspoon red pepper flakes
- 1 tablespoon white wine vinegar
- 1/2 cup extra virgin olive oil
- 500g pasta of your choice
- 1 cup frozen peas

METHOD

1. For the pesto, add the herbs, water, garlic, miso, lemon zest and juice, sugar (or agave), cracked pepper, sea salt, red pepper flakes and vinegar to a high-speed blender. Blend. Push down sides with a spatula and blend again, this time drizzling with olive oil while processing until smooth. Set aside.
2. Bring a large pot of salted water to the boil and cook pasta until almost done. Add frozen peas and boil for one more minute (this will finish cooking the pasta and blanch the peas). Drain everything in a colander. Return the pasta and peas back to the pot and mix in the pesto.
3. Serve hot in your Coconut Bowls or leave the pot in the fridge for a chilled pasta the next day. Add sea salt and black pepper to taste. Garnish with fresh basil and mint leaves.

Tip: To make this dish allergen free, use your favourite gluten-free pasta and substitute sunflower seeds for the nuts. For a soy-free version, use chickpea miso.

Timothy Pakron @mississippivegan
Timothy Pakron, aka Mississippi Vegan, is an American artist, food photographer and stylist, recipe developer and teacher. He currently resides in Jackson, where he is working on his first cookbook due out in Autumn 2018. You can find more recipes by Timothy on his blog mississippivegan.com. In his spare time, Timothy enjoys foraging, gardening and drinking delicious wine.

Smoky Beet & Sweet Potato Burger

Nothing can 'beet' this protein-packed, antioxidant-enriched, flavourful and colourful burger. Made with luscious beets, sweet potato, chickpeas, oats and quinoa, this smoky burger will leave your tastebuds buzzing and your tummy very full.

MAKES 4 BURGERS

INGREDIENTS

Burger
- 2 medium beetroots, chopped
- 1 large sweet potato, chopped
- 1/2 tablespoon avocado oil
- 1/2 teaspoon cayenne pepper
- 1 teaspoon cumin
- 3 garlic cloves, crushed
- 1/2 cup rolled oats
- 2 teaspoons paprika
- 1 cup quinoa, cooked

Hummus
- 1 cup chickpeas
- 2 cloves garlic
- 3 tablespoons lemon juice
- 2 tablespoons olive oil
- 1 tablespoon tahini
- Salt and pepper, to taste
- 1 teaspoon blue spirulina (optional)

To serve
- 4 buns, lettuce cups or wraps

METHOD

1. Pre-heat oven to 200°C and line a tray with baking paper.
2. Toss beetroots and sweet potato in avocado oil and bake for 30 minutes or until soft.
3. Once the beets and sweet potato are soft, place all the ingredients in a high-speed blender and blend to combine.
4. Transfer into a mixing bowl and hand mix to ensure the mixture is well combined.
5. Scoop 1/2 cup of burger mixture to form each patty. This will make 4 burgers.
6. Bake on your prepared tray for 24 minutes, flipping once.
7. Meanwhile, make your hummus. Drain and rinse chickpeas, blend chickpeas in a high-speed blender until smooth. Add in all remaining hummus ingredients and blend well.
8. Throw your burgers in a bun, lettuce cup or wrap. Top with hummus and serve.

Stephanie Tavares & Sam Clark @sugaredcoconut
Steph and Sam are a vegan couple who love to travel, eat and share their plant-based recipes. They live in Toronto, where Steph grew up. Their hobbies and interests include travel, fitness, cooking, photography and videography.

Green Goddess Bowl

*With a combination of all my favourite greens, this bowl has me hooked.
My husband wonders if I'll ever tire of it but I don't think I will – it is truly
that good. The pesto combines effortlessly with the quinoa and avocado
while the fresh salad leaves and seeds give this ultimate brunch the
necessary added texture. The perfect green bowl, fit for a goddess.*

MAKES 3 BOWLS

INGREDIENTS

- 1 cup (90 g) broccoli, sliced
- 1 teaspoon olive oil
- 1 heaped tablespoon pesto
  (you can use store-bought pesto
  or find my five-minute vegan
  pesto on page 256)
- 11/2 cups (270g) pre-cooked
  quinoa, cooled
- 1 avocado, diced
- 2 tablespoons sauerkraut
- 1 zucchini, spiralised
- 1 teaspoon olive oil
- 1/2 lemon, juiced
- 1 tablespoon hemp seeds
- 1 tablespoon pepita seeds
- A few sprigs of basil, to serve
- Lemon wedges, to serve
- Pinch salt and pepper

METHOD

1. Fill a medium saucepan with water and bring to a boil. Add broccoli
   to boiling water and allow to boil for 1 minute or until just tender.
   Remove and cool with iced water. Set aside.
2. Heat the olive oil in a large frying pan over medium heat. Add pesto
   and spread over pan, then add broccoli. Stir briefly.
3. Add quinoa and lemon juice, stir briefly and remove from heat.
4. In a mixing bowl, combine the quinoa mix with avocado, sauerkraut and
   zucchini, then divide the mix between 3 Coconut Bowls.
5. Top with hemp seeds and pepitas, and serve with basil leaves
   and a wedge of lemon. Sprinkle with salt and pepper to taste.

Taline Gabrielian @talinegabriel
Taline is an Australian blogger and the creator of Hippie Lane – a place that inspires the
coming together of people, friends and family over a delicious spread of nourishing food.
Hippie Lane is Taline's way of sharing her passion for health and wellbeing and appreciation
for flavoursome food that nourishes mind, body and soul. Her work has also been translated
into a cookbook and recipe app.

Red Quinoa with Smoky Sweet Pepper Sauce

This bowl is one of my go-to favourites during the week, and it will become one for you too. There are many variations that you can create, the options here are endless. I totally recommend you make extra of everything for a delicious wrap or salad the following day.

MAKES 2 BOWLS

INGREDIENTS

Spicy sweet pepper sauce
- 3 capsicums, halved
- 1/2 cup cashews, soaked for 4 hours
- 1/4 teaspoon garlic powder
- Chilli powder, to taste
- 1/4 teaspoon chipotle pepper
- 6–8 mint leaves
- 1 tablespoon nutritional yeast
- 1/2 teaspoon sea salt
- 1/4 cup water
- Sea salt, to taste

Red quinoa
- 1 small cauliflower, sliced
- 1 teaspoon olive oil
- Salt and pepper, to taste
- 1/2 cup quinoa rinsed
- 1 cup water
- 2 tablespoons beetroot, finely grated
- 100g green beans
- 1/4 cup raw cashews, toasted
- 1 spring onion, finely sliced

METHOD

1. Heat oven to 200°C and line a baking sheet with baking paper.
2. Place capsicums skin-side up on baking sheet. Bake for 20 minutes, or until soft. Set aside to cool.
3. Meanwhile, rinse the soaked cashews.
4. Blend cooled capsicum and cashews with the rest of your sauce ingredients in a high-speed blender until soft and creamy. Set aside.
5. Place cauliflower in a bowl with oil, salt, pepper and toss to coat evenly. Place on baking sheet with the peppers and bake for 20 minutes, or until golden brown.
6. Place quinoa, water, grated beet, a pinch of salt in a small pan. Cover and bring to the boil, reduce the heat and simmer covered for about 10 minutes. Set aside.
7. Cook green beans in hot water or in a steam basket until tender.
8. Assemble quinoa, beans and cauliflower in your Coconut Bowls, drizzle with smoky pepper sauce and top with toasted cashews and spring onions.

Heike Müller @tastyasheck
Heike loves to eat rainbow food all day, every day! The Swiss visual designer lives in the countryside at Lake Zurich, where she grows her own edible blossoms to top her food with. She doesn't have a problem demolishing them with pleasure.

Ratatouille Bowl

There's nothing more French than ratatouille. In the south of France, where I grew up, it is a popular summer recipe and is often eaten hot or cold, served with pasta or rice. This is a family recipe that is been passed down from generation to generation (thanks, Grand-Mère), which I've paired with quinoa and raw vegetables. As a good ratatouille takes quite some time to prepare, this recipe will make a large quantity.

MAKES 6–8 BOWLS

INGREDIENTS

- 5 tablespoons extra virgin olive oil
- 2 white onions, thinly sliced
- 2 red capsicums, seeds removed, finely diced
- 2 eggplants, cut lengthways then into half moons
- 3 cloves garlic, thinly sliced
- 4 very firm courgettes, cut lengthways then into half moons
- 6 medium tomatoes, finely diced
- Salt and pepper
- 1/4 teaspoon cayenne pepper
- 1 tablespoon thyme
- 4 teaspoons coconut sugar, plus extra to taste
- Handful of basil leaves
- Extra vegetables, to serve
- Cooked quinoa, rice or pasta, to serve

METHOD

1. Pour olive oil into a large casserole pan. Add the onions and the capsicums and saute over a high heat for 15 minutes. Then add eggplant, garlic and courgettes. Stir with a wooden spoon and cook for another 10 minutes before adding the tomatoes.
2. Season with salt, pepper, cayenne pepper and thyme. Add the sugar, adjusting according to the acidity of the tomatoes. Stir and lower the heat.
3. Simmer over a very low heat, without covering, for at least 2 1/2 hours.
4. At the end of cooking, add a few basil leaves and stir.
5. Wait until it cools down, then serve in your Coconut Bowls with any veggies you like and a base of quinoa, rice or pasta.

Tip: Depending on the season, the vegetables may hold more or less water when simmering. If the vegetables give a lot of water during cooking, don't hesitate to remove excess water with a spoon. Store extra ratatouille in an airtight container in the fridge for 4 to 5 days.

Eva Gaillot @thefrenchcoconut
Eva is The French Coconut. She's a vegan recipe developer, coconut lover and storyteller from the south of France. You will hear her talking about all things healthy, including lifestyle, plant-based food and good vibes.

Roasted Gnocchi with Avocado Cream

Good gnocchi takes time – this is great gnocchi, and worth every second of effort. Roasting the gnocchi with juicy tomatoes creates an incredible aroma and crispness, making it all the more delicious. Avocado cream with pine nuts and basil completes this dish perfectly.

MAKES 2 BOWLS

INGREDIENTS

Gnocchi
- 400g potatoes
- 150g flour, plus extra for covering
- 1 tablespoon oil, to roast

Avocado cream
- 1 ripe avocado
- 20g pine nuts, toasted
- Juice of 1/2 lime
- Fresh basil
- 1 clove garlic
- Nutmeg, to taste
- Salt and pepper, to taste

To serve
- 150g cherry tomatoes, sliced
- Salt and pepper

METHOD

1. Cook the whole potatoes until tender. Peel the warm potatoes and press them with a potato ricer on your benchtop. Add flour and knead it until you have a smooth dough. Add more flour if the dough sticky. Cover the dough and set aside for 15 minutes.
2. Cut the dough into 4 parts and roll each to a long sausage shape. Use flour to cover the dough and your bench top. Cut into small, gnocchi-sized pieces.
3. Put your gnocchi in salted boiled water and cook them until they are swimming on the top. Remove from water an set aside while you make your avocado cream.
4. Blend avocado, pine nuts, lime juice, basil, garlic and spices in a blender until creamy.
5. Roast the drained gnocchi for 5–10 minutes in oil and add sliced tomatoes. Serve in your Coconut Bowls, smother with your avocado cream and season with salt and pepper.

Ronja Pfuhl @miss_gruenkern
Ronja is a food photographer from Germany. Though food photography is her job and she loves it, it is not her only passion. She also loves to share delicious pictures of her own recipes. Ronja runs Food 'n' Photo workshops, as well as her blog and magazine.

Creamy Kale & Pea Risotto

*The combination of nutritional yeast and tahini gives this delicious, creamy
risotto a rich cheesy flavour without using butter, cheese or cream. Perfect
as a post-workout lunch or warm, hearty dinner.*

MAKES 2 BOWLS

INGREDIENTS

- 1 clove garlic, minced
- 1 brown onion, diced
- 1 tablespoon coconut oil
- 1 cup arborio rice
- 2 cups vegetable stock
- 1 tablespoon tahini
- 2 tablespoons nutritional yeast,
  plus extra to serve
- 1/2 cup green peas, steamed
- Handful of curly kale, shredded

METHOD

1. Add the garlic, onion and oil to a pot over medium heat
   and stir until onion becomes translucent.
2. Stir in rice and toast for 1–2 minutes, or until rice is well coated
   and slightly glossy.
3. Add stock1/4cup at a time, stirring constantly until absorbed.
4. Remove from heat and stir through tahini, nutritional yeast,
   peas and kale.
5. Add an extra sprinkle of nutritional yeast and serve into
   your Coconut Bowls.

Tip: Double the recipe to enjoy plenty of leftovers the next day.

Elizabeth Gageler @cheekycoconuts
Elizabeth was born in Canberra, grew up on Sydney's north shore and now lives on the
golden sands of Bondi Beach. Elizabeth works in corporate marketing and her hobbies include
weightlifting and cooking. She is passionate about living a chemical-free lifestyle and showing
people how to incorporate essential oils into their daily lives for ultimate health and wellness.

Mexican Fiesta Bowl

This is a perfect fiesta dish. It is an explosion of Mexican flavours and textures: creamy guacamole meets spicy beans and crispy potatoes. Yum!

MAKES 2 BOWLS

INGREDIENTS

- 500g yellow potatoes, sliced

Salsa
- 1/2 tomato, finely chopped
- 1/3 cup fresh coriander, finely chopped
- 1/3 red onion, finely chopped
- 1 avocado, mashed
- 1 tablespoon lime juice

Bean Chilli
- 225g low-sodium kidney beans, drained
- 400g crushed tomatoes
- 1 tablespoon cumin
- 1 teaspoon smoked paprika
- 1/8 teaspoon cayenne

To Serve
- 1/2 cup unsweetened coconut yoghurt
- Fresh coriander

METHOD

1. Pre-heat oven to 200°C. Place potatoes on an oven tray lined with baking paper. Bake for approximately 15 minutes or until lightly browned.
2. To make salsa, combine the tomato, coriander, onion, avocado and the lime juice in a large bowl. Set aside.
3. Make the bean chilli by putting the beans, crushed tomatoes, cumin, smoked paprika and cayenne in a pan. Simmer on medium heat for about 10 minutes, or until the mixture thickens.
4. Place the potatoes, salsa and bean chilli in your Coconut Bowls and garnish with coconut yoghurt and coriander.

Alexandra Andersson @fivesechealth
Alexandra was born and raised in southern Sweden. While she still lives in Sweden, her dreams are elsewhere. Alexandra's passion is to inspire people to live a healthy lifestyle that benefits not only ourselves, but our planet and animals. Together with her brand Fivesec Health, Alexandra believes we can change the world.

Lime & Potato Curry

This is a great recipe when you are in a hurry, but want something to give you those comfort feels. We all love a good curry, and this is one you can make with ingredients already in your pantry.

MAKES 2 BOWLS

INGREDIENTS

- 1 tablespoon olive oil
- 1 clove garlic, finely chopped
- 1 onion or shallot, finely chopped
- 1 large potato, chopped
- 1 small eggplant, chopped
- 1 tablespoon curry powder
- 400ml coconut milk
- Salt and pepper

To Serve
- Coconut yoghurt
- Fresh coriander
- Toasted cashews
- Black sesame seeds
- 1 lime wedge

METHOD

1. In a medium-sized pan, heat the olive oil and fry garlic and onions until translucent.
2. Add the rest of your veggies along with the curry powder and coconut milk. Simmer, covered, for 20 minutes. Season to taste.
3. When your 20 minutes are up you will have a nice creamy mixture of curry goodness. Scoop into your Coconut Bowls and top with coconut yoghurt, fresh coriander, toasted cashews, sesame seeds and a lime wedge.

Tip: Double the recipe to enjoy plenty of leftovers the next day.

Bettina Campolucci Bordi @bettinas_kitchen
Bettina says she began blogging because "most people have no idea how good their body is designed to feel". Turning vegan was a significant moment in her life, and sparked a love affair with creativity and ingredients, their heritage and ways to use them. There is so much beauty in this world in the form of nature. Bettina aspires to spread it as far is it can reach.

Coconut Rice & Edamame Bowl

Prepare for a rush of happiness when you try this bowl. Fresh salad, sweet coconut rice and a blueberry in every mouthful, this guilt-free recipe is one to savour.

MAKES 2 BOWLS

INGREDIENTS

Bowl
- 1 cup brown rice
- 2 cups water
- 1 teaspoon garlic powder
- 1 tablespoon apple cider or rice vinegar
- 1/2 tablespoon coconut sugar
- 1 tablespoon tamari sauce
- 4 tablespoons coconut milk
- 1/2 cup fresh or frozen peas
- 1/2 cup frozen edamame
- Pinch of salt

Toppings
- 1 carrot, spiralised
- 1/2 cucumber, spiralised
- 1/2 small avocado, sliced
- 1 handful blueberries
- Juice of 1 lime
- 2 teaspoons black sesames

METHOD

1. Rinse the brown rice well. Combine with water and garlic powder in a medium pot. Cover and let the rice cook until all the water has absorbed, 45 minutes.
2. Whisk together the vinegar, coconut sugar, tamari sauce and coconut milk, then stir into the cooked rice.
3. While the rice cooks, prepare the vegetables. Boil edamame and peas in water with a dash of salt for three minutes.
4. Once the rice is done, serve in your Coconut Bowls and top with all the veggies and blueberries. Serve with sesame seeds, lime and extra tamari sauce if needed.

Annelina Waller @annelinawaller
Annelina from Germany is a recipe creator, food blogger and author of the best-selling book, *Buddha Bowls*. Her goal is to inspire people to become the happiest they've ever been. Her heart beats for simple plant-based and raw food. She loves to share simple vegan recipes and the way to healthy, conscious living with you.

Momo Pêche Bento Bowl

A harmonious explosion of flavours, textures and nutrients! Momo means 'peach' in Japanese, and bento is a packed lunch made up from rice and lots of small dishes. In the Momo Pêche Bowl, soft grilled peach is best friends with tangy quick pickles, fragrant crushed sesame seed, bitter leaves and comforting beans. The dishes can be prepared ahead so everyone can have fun filling their own bowls at lunch or dinner time.

MAKES 2 BOWLS

INGREDIENTS

- 1 carrot, cut into long ribbons (I used a mix of purple and orange carrot)
- 1 tablespoon brown rice vinegar
- 150g cooked cannellini beans (or any large white bean)
- 1/2 cucumber, core removed and cut into bite-sized chunks
- 2 tablespoons light miso paste
- Juice of 1/2 organic lemon, plus a little grated zest
- 4 tablespoons sesame seeds
- 1/2 teaspoon good-quality salt
- 1 peach, halved
- 1/2 avocado, sliced
- 1 raddicchio, thinly sliced (or another bitter salad leaf)
- 2 cups cooked grains, to serve (I used brown short-grain rice)
- 1 pinch gochugaru (Korean pepper) or chilli flakes, to garnish (optional)

METHOD

1. Start by making quick pickled carrots, tossing the carrot with vinegar. Set aside. The longer they rest the better. Quick pickle can be kept for a week or more in the fridge.
2. Make smashed beans by adding beans, cucumber, miso, lemon juice and zest to a large glass jar. Close tightly with a lid and give it a good shake. Taste test and add more miso paste or salt as needed. Leave to rest for at least 15 minutes. Smashed beans last for up to 2 days in the fridge.
3. Prepare the gomashio (sesame salt). Toast sesame seeds in a dry pan until fragrant. Grind with a mortar and pestle, leaving some seeds whole. If you don't have a pestle just crush them with the back of a wooden spoon against a cutting board.
4. Grill the peaches, without oil, in a grill pan or normal frying pan over a high heat, 1–2 minutes each side.
5. To serve, make a bed of grains in each Coconut Bowl. Add the pickle, smashed beans, peach, avocado and raddichio in separate sections and finish with a couple of spoonfuls of gomashio in the middle and a sprinkling of gochugaru, if using.

Sara Kiyo Popowa @shisodelicious
Sara of Shiso Delicious is a London-based blogger and food photographer, bringing her colourful, multicultural twist on plant-based food wherever she goes! Her food philosophy is anchored in organic food, reducing waste in the community, and in loving ourselves as well as the world around us. You may have seen her packed lunches on Instagram, where she sometimes goes by the name, Queen of Bento.

Plant-Based Spaghetti & Meatballs

It is time for spaghetti and meatballs! Vegan meatballs, of course, made with lentils. This delicious yet unusual take on an Italian classic will shoot to the top of your regulars list. It is so good your non-vegan friends will enjoy it too.

MAKES 2 BOWLS

INGREDIENTS

- 2 zucchinis
- 40g quinoa, rinsed
- 80g water
- 40g sunflower seeds, shelled in water
- 150g canned lentils, drained
- 2 teaspoons garlic powder
- 2 teaspoons dried Italian herbs, plus extra for seasoning
- 15g fresh basil
- 1 1/2 onions, finely chopped
- 250ml canned tomatoes
- Salt and pepper

METHOD

1. Pre-heat your oven on 180°C.
2. Using a spiraliser, make spaghetti from the zucchini and set aside.
3. In a medium-sized pot, add quinoa and water. Bring to a boil and cook for 10–12 minutes. Drain and set aside.
4. Grind the sunflower seeds in a high-speed blender and place in a large bowl. Add the lentils, garlic powder, Italian herbs, half of the fresh basil and the freshly cut onion. Also add the cooked quinoa and season with some salt and pepper.
5. Knead the mixture with your hands and form into 4 large or 8 small balls.
6. Place the balls on an oven tray lined with baking paper. Transfer to the oven and bake the balls for about 10 minutes, until crispy and brown. Keep an eye on them, turning halfway.
7. In the meantime, make the tomato sauce by heating up the tomatoes in a pan. Season with Italian herbs and remaining basil.
8. Add the balls to your sauce and cook briefly until heated through.
9. Serve over a bed of the spaghetti in your Coconut Bowls.

Merel von Carlsberg & Tessa Moorman @thegreenhappiness
Merel and Tessa are The Green Happiness. Based in Amsterdam, the pair has developed multiple healthy recipe books, including summer and winter editons of *Your 50 Days of Green Happiness*. Their mission is to inspire others to eat healthier and to feel happier, sexier and more energetic, giving them a genuine glow. All through plant-based food.

Sweets

CHAPTER 04

DESSERTS - RAW TREATS

Sweets

Keep your heart shining and your mouth smiling with these delicious desserts and raw treats.

Sweet and indulgent doesn't have to mean guilty and unhealthy. We believe there's no better time to treat yourself than the present, so pack a pantry full of your favourite flavours for whenever hunger strikes.

We like to think of coconut, cacao, nuts and dates as your best friends here. Go on, let your heart guide you as you design your next sweet treat.

Energy boosting bliss balls are like happy pills and an endorphin rush. Simple to make and long lasting, these little bundles of joy can be made with any ingredients you desire – the choice is yours!

Dessert is good for your soul, so embrace your inner sweet tooth and remember, when the question is chocolate related, the answer is always yes.

Pandan Coconut Ice-Cream

This is a dessert inspired by my Malaysian heritage. Growing up, lots of my favourite desserts would be flavoured with pandan. Pandan is often described as the Asian version of vanilla and pairs perfectly with coconut. This smooth and creamy vegan ice cream can be scooped straight out of the freezer.

MAKES 8 BOWLS

INGREDIENTS

- 400ml full fat coconut cream
- 3/4 cup coconut sugar
- 1 tablespoon cornflower
- 1 tablespoon lukewarm water
- Pinch of salt
- 3 teaspoons pandan essence (you can find this at your local Asian grocery shop)

METHOD

1. Add the coconut cream and sugar into a pot over medium heat and stir until sugar is dissolved.
2. In a small separate bowl, mix the cornflour with the water to create a cornstarch slurry.
3. Add the slurry, salt and the pandan essence into the coconut cream mixture and mix until it is nice and thick.
4. Remove from heat and allow to cool to room temperature before chilling in the fridge for at least 8 hours.
5. Pour the mixture into an ice-cream churner, and churn for about 20–30 minutes.
6. Scoop the mixture into a freezer safe container and freeze for at least another 3 hours before serving in your Coconut Bowls.

Tip: If you don't have an ice-cream churner, pour the chilled mixture into a freezer-safe container. Freeze for 2–3 hours, stirring the mixture every 30 minutes. This adds air to the mixture and helps it become creamier. After this step, the mixture can be left to harden completely.

Stephanie Young @rainbowsforbreakfast_
Steph is from sunny Queensland, Australia. Although she loves leading a healthy lifestyle, like most of us, Steph also has a massive sweet tooth. Her motto is moderation not deprivation. She is the foodie and girlboss behind the superfood company, Just Blends.

Blueberry Lime Blissies

*These colourful little bliss balls are perfect when you crave something
sweet, yet healthy. Filled with antioxidants from the blueberries,
and easy to make, these are a crowd pleaser for any occasion.*

MAKES 10-12 BALLS

INGREDIENTS

- 2 teaspoons lime zest,
  plus extra for rolling
- 1/3 cup of shredded coconut,
  plus extra for rolling
- 20 dates, pitted and soaked
- 1 cup blueberries
- 2 cups oats
- 2 teaspoons vanilla bean powder

METHOD

1. Combine lime zest and shredded coconut flakes in a bowl.
2. Mix the rest of the ingredients with your hands in a bigger bowl
   and roll into balls.
3. Roll each ball in lime zest and coconut until totally covered
   and place in your Coconut Bowls, ready to serve.

*Tip: If you're using fresh blueberries, place the balls in the fridge
for a while to set. If using frozen blueberries, let them defrost first
so they are not too cold to work with.*

Victoria Rosell @inspiredbyvic
Victoria grew up surrounded by nature in the countryside of Sweden. Food is Victoria's
biggest interest, and her passion is to be creative in the kitchen while inspiring others to do
the same, through positive vibes and plant-based whole foods.

Raw Mint-Choc Truffles

Looking for an easy, nutritious, amazingly delicious and indulgent crowd pleaser? These chocolate mint truffles are just what you're looking for. These are so much better than regular truffles. They are fully raw and contain only healthy ingredients. Enjoy with friends, family or even just treat yourself.

MAKES 12+ TRUFFLES

INGREDIENTS

- 1 cup coconut, shredded
- Pinch of salt
- 10 Medjool dates
- 2 tablespoons almond butter
- 4 tablespoons raw cacao powder, plus extra for coating
- 1/2 teaspoon peppermint extract (or 2 drops food-grade peppermint essential oil)

METHOD

1. Place coconut and salt in a blender and blend until finely ground.
2. Add the dates, almond butter, cacao powder, peppermint and process until the mixture starts to stick together.
3. Using about a tablespoon of the mixture, roll into balls.
4. Roll each ball in cacao powder and store in the fridge until firm.

Tip: You can also coat your truffles in cacao nibs or matcha green tea powder.

Cailin Grant-Jansen @caiirose
Cailin is an Aussie-Belgian trying to live her dream life. From a young age, Cailin knew she would not stay in the one place forever. After studying Arabic and living in Morocco for a year, travelling helped open her eyes to how much beauty is in this world. After struggling to find her own path, Cailin became determined to live more in the moment and to develop a healthy plant-based lifestyle.

Matcha Ice-Cream with Mint Pesto & Pineapple

This is the perfect summer dessert. Exotic flavours and healthy ingredients are combined to make an easy, no-churn vegan ice-cream that will make your tastebuds happy. It is a must try for all matcha lovers!

MAKES 2 BOWLS

INGREDIENTS

Ice-Cream
- 200ml aquafaba (chickpea water)
- 400ml full-fat coconut milk
- 2 teaspoons vanilla extract
- 5 tablespoons maple syrup
- 2 teaspoons matcha powder
- 2 passionfruit, flesh removed

Pesto
- 1 bunch mint, washed and leaves removed
- Zest and juice of 1 lime
- 4 tablespoons raw cane sugar (or coconut sugar)
- 30g pistachios (roasted and salted)
- 2 tablespoons coconut syrup

Grilled Pineapple
- 1/2 fresh pineapple, sliced
- 2 tablespoons lime juice
- 1 tablespoon coconut sugar
- 1 tablespoon coconut oil, melted

METHOD

Ice-Cream
1. Chill the coconut milk in the fridge overnight.
2. Beat the aquafaba in a high-speed blender until firm. Add the hardened part of the chilled coconut milk to the fluffy aquafaba, along with the vanilla, maple syrup and matcha. Mix until well combined.
3. Transfer to a freezer-safe pan and stir through the passionfruit.
4. Freeze overnight. No need to stir.

Pesto
5. Tip all ingredients into a blender and mix until well combined.

Grilled Pineapple
6. Drizzle pineapple with lime juice.
7. Heat a pan, brush pineapple with coconut oil and sprinkle with sugar.
8. Grill for 2–3 minutes on both sides.

To Serve
9. Take out the ice-cream and leave to soften outside for 10–15 minutes before serving. Add to your Coconut Bowls, drizzle with the pesto and serve with the grilled pineapple on top.

Verena Frei @frei_style
Freistyle – that is Verena, a Switzerland-based mum of twins. Freistyle is a food, travel and lifestyle blog where Verena shares her passion for healthy food and plant-based recipes. Verena also talks about her other passions, such as travelling with her family, styling, photography and living a healthy and sustainable lifestyle.

Chocolate Peanut Butter Protein Balls

These protein packed energy balls are perfect on-the-go snacks for busy bees. They make amazing toppings for smoothie bowls, while also satisfying your sweet cravings in between meals. Why not prepare them for the week ahead?

MAKES 12+ BALLS

INGREDIENTS

- Handful of almonds
- 1/2 cup oats
- 1 scoop vegan chocolate protein powder
- 1/2 teaspoon cinnamon
- 1 teaspoon coconut oil
- 6–7 pitted dates, soaked in hot water to soften
- 1 tablespoon smooth peanut butter
- 1 tablespoon cacao powder, plus extra to coat
- 1 tablespoon chia seeds, plus extra to coat

METHOD

1. In a high-speed blender, blitz almonds and oats until the mixture achieves a flour-like consistency.
2. Add remaining ingredients and blend until the mixture forms into dough. Aim for a crumbly and sticky consistency.
3. Roll the dough into balls and coat with chia seeds, cacao powder, or as desired.
4. Chill for 30 minutes to an hour to set before serving.

Tip: Store in an airtight container and enjoy through the week.

Cheptoo Chirchir @mynuttydelights
Cheptoo is originally from Kenya and has lived in the United Kingdom for the past four years studying at the University of Leeds. She believes in starting your morning with a good workout and a delicious nutritious breakfast to keep you going throughout the day.

Choc-Cherry Raspberry Bites

This is a light and sweet coconut treat with a hint of cherry. Lathered with vegan chocolate, these bites will satisfy those sweet cravings the moment they hit your lips.

MAKES 12+ BITES

INGREDIENTS

- 2 cups desiccated coconut
- 2 tablespoons coconut oil
- 1 cup fresh or frozen cherries
- 1 teaspoon maple syrup
- 1/2 teaspoon vanilla
- 1 cup frozen raspberries
- 1/4 cup black chia seeds
- 1 tablespoon stevia (or sugar of your choice)
- 2 cups vegan chocolate buttons
- 2 tablespoons coconut oil

METHOD

1. Put desiccated coconut, coconut oil, cherries, maple syrup and vanilla into a blender. Blend on high to combine.
2. Line a cake pan with baking paper. Add coconut cherry mixture and flatten with spoon. Set aside.
3. To make the jam filling, heat raspberries, chia and sweetener in a saucepan over medium heat. Simmer while stirring for 5 minutes, or until the mixture is syrup-like. Keep watch and stir often as the jam can burn easily.
4. Spread jam on top of the coconut cherry mixture then place in freezer for at least 1 hour.
5. Melt chocolate with coconut oil over a low heat. Once melted, pour into a bowl and set aside.
6. Remove coconut cherry from freezer and cut with a hot knife into bite-sized pieces.
7. Dip your coconut cherry pieces into the chocolate with a fork and place on baking paper in the fridge to set.

Mellissa Byrne @one_full_belly
Mellissa is a mum of two girls and works fulltime as a registered nurse. She began her plant-based journey to regain health, and fit as much goodness into her busy lifestyle as possible. Originally from the Snowy Mountains, Mellissa now resides in the far north coast of New South Wales, where she enjoys camping and exploring all the wonderful food that is on offer in this region.

Midnight Energy Balls

Midnight Energy Balls are a healthy and delicious snack for any time of day. Made with creamy nut butter, coconut flakes and cacao powder, they're a rich, chocolatey treat that is also low in sugar. Best enjoyed before or after workouts, or as a late-night snack.

MAKES 12+ BALLS

INGREDIENTS

- 2/3 cup toasted coconut flakes (untoasted works great too)
- 2/3 cup rolled oats
- 1/3 cup almond butter (or a vegan butter of your choice)
- 2–3 tablespoons raw cacao powder
- 3 tablespoons coconut oil
- 3 tablespoons nut milk
- 1/3 cup Medjool dates, pitted
- 1 teaspoon vanilla powder or extract
- Pinch of salt

METHOD

1. Add all ingredients to your high-speed blender and blend until smooth.
2. Roll the mixture into small balls.
3. Store in your fridge.

Tip: Try rolling in coconut flakes before serving.

Marie Reginato @marie.reginato
Marie is a California-based wellness writer, photographer and cooking video host. She focuses on delicious recipes that also happen to be good for you. Marie is featured on the leading wellness site, MindBodyGreen, as one of the Best Healthy Food Accounts, and will soon be releasing her first cookbook, *Alternative Vegan*.

Watermelon Coconut Sorbet

This is the ultimate healthy summer sorbet. The blend of watermelon and coconut creates the most refreshing flavour that you could ever imagine.

MAKES 4 BOWLS

INGREDIENTS

- 8 cups watermelon chunks
- 2 cups coconut milk
- 1/2 teaspoon vanilla extract

METHOD

1. Tip all ingredients into your high-speed blender and pulse until smooth.
2. Place into a container and freeze for 3 hours.
3. Remove from freezer, then break up and stir mixture so that it doesn't harden like one big ice block.
4. Freeze again and, when you're ready to eat, remove from freezer and let sit for 15 minutes before serving.
5. Scoop the sorbet into your Coconut Bowls.

Neto Rivas @therawboy
Neto is a raw vegan recipe developer from Texas, in the United States. Just one look at his YouTube feed, The Raw Boy, will leave your mouth watering. You can enjoy all of Neto's recipe creations in both English and Spanish.

Coconut Twix-Style Bars

These healthy raw vegan bars are an alternative to the famous Twix bar, which you might remember from your childhood. One bite of these and you won't believe they are gluten free, refined sugar free and vegan.

MAKES 10–12 BARS

INGREDIENTS

Filling

- 2 tablespoons agave syrup
- 2/3 cup coconut flour
- 1/4 cup extra virgin coconut oil, melted and cooled
- 3 tablespoons full-fat coconut milk
- 14 Medjool dates, pitted
- 1/4 stick vegan butter
- 1 tablespoon blackstrap molasses
- 1 teaspoon vanilla extract

Chocolate Coating

- 1 cup (150g) dark chocolate
- 2 tablespoons coconut oil
- 1 tablespoon full-fat coconut milk

METHOD

Filling

1. For the crust, combine agave syrup, coconut flour, coconut oil and 2 tablespoons of the coconut mik in a medium-sized bowl. With your fingers, press into a rectangular container or tin.
2. For the caramel, use a high-speed blender and combine the dates with the butter, remaining coconut milk, molasses and vanilla.
3. Pour over crust and place the dish in the freezer while you are making the chocolate.

Chocolate Coating

4. In a small pot, melt the dark chocolate and coconut oil over a low heat until melted. Slowly add the coconut milk and stir until combined. Pour the chocolate over the filling.

To Serve

5. Freeze for at least 30 minutes before cutting into bars and serving.

Lara Zaugg @vanillacrunnch
Lara is a passionate food and lifestyle blogger from Switzerland. She is also a cat and art lover. Lara loves to experiment in the kitchen creating new desserts, sometimes baked and sometimes raw. Her blog vanillacrunnch.com takes you inside the magical world of vegan desserts.

White & Dark Chocolate Ube Cheesecakes

What to do when you're craving cake, but don't want to turn on the oven? The answer: raw vegan cheesecake. Antioxidant-rich purple ube, white chocolate and raw cacao powder combine to form crustless, vegan cheesecakes that will have you begging for more.

MAKES 2 BOWLS

INGREDIENTS

Purple Ube Layer

- 2 cups soaked cashews, soaked
- 1/2 cup coconut milk
- 1 cup ube (purple sweet potato), peeled
- 2 tablespoons cacao butter
- 1/4 teaspoon vanilla bean paste
- 2 tablespoons pure maple syrup

Chocolate Layer

- 2 cups soaked cashews
- 1/2 cup coconut milk
- 2 tablespoons cacao butter, melted
- 1/4 teaspoon vanilla bean paste
- 3 tablespoons pure maple syrup
- 3 teaspoon raw cacao powder

METHOD

1. For the purple ube layer, combine all ingredients in a high-speed blender and blend until smooth and creamy. Set aside.
2. For the chocolate layer, combine all ingredients except the cacao powder in a high-speed blender and blend until smooth and creamy.
3. Evenly divide the chocolate layer into 2 mixing bowls and add 3 teaspoons of cacao powder to one of the bowls.
4. Mix each bowl with a spoon until fully combined and the cream is completely smooth (you don't want any cacao chunks).
5. Pour half of the purple ube cream into a Coconut Bowl and add the white chocolate cream. Set aside some purple ube cream to decorate.
6. For the dark chocolate cheesecake, repeat the same process by layering the purple ube cream with dark chocolate cream in a Coconut Bowl.
7. To decorate, use a sandwich or piping bag to apply the remaining cream to the cheesecakes.
8. Chill in the freezer for about 2 hours to set – no baking needed.

Zoe Raissakis @wildblend
Zoe is a CrossFitter and wellness blogger from Brisbane, Australia. Her label, Wildblend, aims to inspire people to live an active, happy and healthy lifestyle, and to eat raw, natural foods to nourish their bodies and their souls. Her recipes are focused on fresh seasonal ingredients and celebrate unprocessed, healthy wholefoods.

Mango Lime Nice-Cream

*What's not to love about nice-cream? This combo of frozen mango,
bananas and lime juice blends into a delicious guilt-free soft serve.
The maple syrup adds the hint of sweetness that we all crave
with ice-cream.*

MAKES 2 BOWLS

INGREDIENTS

Nice-Cream
- 4 frozen bananas
- 1 cup frozen mangos
- 1 1/2 tablespoons maple syrup
- 2 tablespoons lime juice
- 1/4 cup water

Toppings
- Fresh fruit, nuts and seeds,
  to serve (such as bananas,
  strawberries, kiwifruit, mango,
  frozen blueberries and sprouted
  sunflower seeds)

METHOD

1. Add all the ingredients to a high-speed blender and blitz until smooth.
2. Pour into two Coconut Bowls.
3. Top with fresh fruit, nuts and seeds.

*Tip: For a perfectly smooth texture, let the frozen bananas and mango
sit on your kitchen bench for about 15 minutes before blending. The fruit
should still be frozen, but softened slightly. This reduces the amount of
water needed and produces a soft and creamy ice-cream texture.*

Fabiola Femmoe @shinewithplants
Fabiola is French with African roots, now living in Chicago with her family. She is a young
mum who thrives on a natural and mostly raw vegan diet. Fabiola knows what it is like to
feel sick, to feel overweight and in poor physical condition. That is why she wants to share
everything that she has learned to help anyone looking to improve their life, starting with
some positive health changes. Be inspired on Fabiola's blog shinewithplants.com.

Power-Packed Energy Balls

These delicious energising balls are packed with nature's sweetness. They are so simple and quick to make, combining just a handful of ingredients into a snack perfect for a midday nibble. Whether you're looking for something to tide you over until dinner, or something to satisfy those sweet cravings, these energy balls will certainly keep your taste buds happy.

MAKES 12+ BALLS

INGREDIENTS

- 200g fresh or dried dates, pitted
- 1 tablespoon cacao powder
- 2 tablespoons fresh mint, finely chopped (optional)
- 140g rolled oats, plus extra for coating
- 1/4 cup shredded coconut, for coating (optional)

METHOD

1. Blend the dates in a high-speed blender with a splash of warm water until a jammy texture is achieved. To make chocolate mint balls, add cacao and mint.
2. Pour in the oats slowly and blend until the texture resembles cookie dough. You might need to add more warm water to assist with the blending process, but be careful not to add too much, as the mixture may become wet and sticky.
3. Partition the mixture evenly and roll into balls.
4. Roll the balls in shredded coconut or oats until evenly coated and place in the fridge to set.

Tip: Try adding extra shredded coconut to the balls when blending.

Holly Gabrielle @veganhollyg
Born and raised in the United Kingdom, Holly dreams of one day living in the sunny tropics. She transitioned to veganism overnight in 2016, which transformed her mental and physical health. Holly wants to see her generation make wiser and more conscious food and lifestyle choices, while also making steps towards saving this planet and ending animal cruelty. She promotes this vision with her YouTube channel, Holly Gabrielle.

Rainbow Nice-Cream

This pineapple-based green smoothie bowl makes a nourishing and satisfying breakfast with a tropical touch. Spinach and kale are naturally rich in protein and a vast variety of micronutrients make this meal the perfect breakfast or post-workout treat.

MAKES 4 BOWLS

INGREDIENTS

- 6 bananas, chopped and frozen

Mango Nice-Cream
- 1 mango, chopped and frozen
- Juice of 1/2 lime
- 3 tablespoons coconut milk

Blue Nice-Cream
- 1/2 teaspoon blue spirulina powder
- 1 tablespoon vegan protein powder
- 3 tablespoons coconut milk

Raspberry Nice-Cream
- Handful of raspberries, frozen
- Splash of coconut milk

Açai Nice-Cream
- 1 tablespoon açai powder
- Handful of blueberries
- 1 teaspoon vegan protein powder
- 3 tablespoons coconut milk

METHOD

1. Divide bananas into 4 portions.
2. Blend 1 portion with the mango nice-cream ingredients. Set aside in a separate bowl.
3. Repeat for each flavour of nice-cream.
4. Transfer 1/4 of each nice-cream flavour into a Coconut Bowl and swirl it together to make your rainbow nice-cream.

Tip: Add more coconut milk where required to ensure a smooth nice-cream blend. If you cannot source any of these ingredients, simply replace with a handful of spinach or kale and make green nice-cream.

Luisa Gaffga @lulusdreamtown
Lulu is a teenage vegan Instagram and YouTube blogger who is addicted to everything sweet. She is all about beautiful pictures and inspiring people to make positive changes. She promotes self-love, body positivity and general happiness.

Chia Coconut Bliss Balls

This recipe is for anyone who loves coconuts and snacks – so, everybody. The refreshing combination of coconut, chia seeds and lemon tastes delicious, while the possibilities for adaptation are endless, letting you create your own 'perfect' bliss ball.

MAKES 6+ BALLS

INGREDIENTS

- 60g coconut flakes
- 30g oat flour
- 1 heaped tablespoon chia seeds
- 1 splash of lemon juice
- 60g coconut oil
- 4 heaped tablespoons maple syrup
- Cacao, matcha powder, chia seeds or coconut flakes, to coat

METHOD

1. Mix the coconut flakes, oat flour and the chia seeds in a bowl.
2. Add the lemon, coconut oil and maple syrup. Mix and knead with your hands to combine.
3. Form the bliss balls and roll in your desired coating(s).
4. Place in the fridge to set.

Davina Klevinghaus @dav_fitness.food
Davina is a passionate food and fitness blogger from Germany. She's addicted to fruits, vegetables and nuts – especially coconuts (just one of the many reasons why we love her). Davina loves to travel and plans on experiencing as many different cultures as possible.

Fruit Yoghurt Pops

*A cold treat that can be eaten as a quick breakfast or a yummy snack.
These ice pops have all of the breakfast essentials: sweet yoghurt, fresh
fruit and crunchy granola!*

MAKES 6 POPS

INGREDIENTS

- 1/4 cup almond milk
- 500g coconut yoghurt
- 1/4 cup blueberries
- 1 kiwifruit, sliced
- 1/4 cup raspberries
- 1/2 cup granola of choice

METHOD

1. Blend together the almond milk and yoghurt.
2. Take your ice pop moulds and begin filling them with the blended mixture and fruit, alternating between the two. Repeat this process until the moulds are full, finishing with the blended yoghurt mixture.
3. Add granola on top of the yoghurt and add the ice pop sticks. Freeze for 4–6 hours.
4. To serve, run under hot water and pull the pops from the moulds.

Dominique Evans @theveganfiesta
Dominique was born and raised in Washington DC and is currently studying design.
She is passionate about ethical and wholesome living, along with anything that has to do
with art – especially illustration! In her spare time, you can find Dominique creating her own
artwork. Whether through pencil art or painting, she always keeps the creativity flowing.

Chocolate Chip Cookie Dough Ice-Cream Truffles

These delicious ice-cream truffles are the perfect snack-sized not-so-guilty pleasure. They're not only refreshing, but also have a rich, chocolatey crunch that will surely satisfy your sweet tooth. They're also packed with healthy fats and loads of nutrients!

MAKES 8+ TRUFFLES

INGREDIENTS

Cookie Dough
- 2 cups raw cashews
- 1 cup almond milk
- 1/4 cup maple syrup
- 1/4 cup coconut oil
- 1 teaspoon vanilla bean paste
- 1/2 cup vegan chocolate chips (or to your liking)

Chocolate Coating
- 1/2 cup cacao butter
- 1/2 cup unsweetened cocoa powder
- 3 tablespoons maple syrup

METHOD

1. Place cashews and almond milk into your high-speed blender and blend until creamy. Add maple syrup, coconut oil and vanilla bean paste and blend again until mixed well.
2. Pour creamy mixture into a loaf tin (or anything you can easily scoop from) and add chocolate chips. Fold into mixture.
3. Place in freezer for 2–4 hours or until firm enough to scoop and roll into balls.
4. While waiting for the mixture to chill, melt cacao butter on the stove over a low heat.
5. Add cocoa powder and maple syrup to the cacao butter and stir well. Set aside and allow to cool for 10–15 minutes.
6. When the cookie dough is firm enough, scoop and roll into balls then dip into chocolate. The chocolate should harden right away if your cookie dough is cold enough. If not, put the balls back into the freezer for several minutes before continuing.
7. Store chocolate-coated truffles in the freezer or fridge until ready to eat.

Natalya Hardan @natalyahardan
Natalya is passionate about living a healthy and active lifestyle. Taking care of her body and mind are the most important things to her. Natalya is a yoga teacher and personal trainer, and is obsessed with creating healthy vegan desserts. She is currently working on her own recipe book.

Peppermint-Coconut & Maca-Vanilla Creams

*These treats are very simple to make, requiring only a few ingredients.
They also provide some wonderful health benefits and complement
coffee or tea perfectly. They're also perfect for when you just need
a little something to nibble on!*

MAKES 12 BARS

INGREDIENTS

- 2 cups icing sugar,
  plus extra for dusting
- 3 tablespoons maca powder
  (optional)
- 2 1/2 tablespoons coconut
  or vegan butter, melted
- 1/2 teaspoon peppermint
  or vanilla extract
- 1 tablespoon water
- 85g dairy-free dark chocolate
- Desiccated coconut, to coat

METHOD

1. Sift the icing sugar into a large bowl. If using maca powder,
   add this to the icing sugar and mix together.
2. Add the melted butter, peppermint or vanilla extract and water.
   Mix together to form a soft dough. The dough should be thick and
   viscous, not sticky. If it is too wet and runny, add more icing sugar;
   if too dry and solid, add more water.
3. Knead lightly on a surface dusted with icing sugar.
4. Using a rolling pin, roll the mixture out to about 1cm thickness.
   Cut into bars.
5. Place the bars on a lined baking sheet and leave overnight in a cool dry
   place or refrigerator to dry out (do not freeze). Turn them over so they
   dry on both sides.
6. Prepare the chocolate coating by melting the chocolate in a microwave.
   Dip the dried bars in the melted chocolate and coat well.
7. Sprinkle over desiccated coconut and place back on the lined baking
   sheet. Leave to set in the fridge.

Lauren Mackenzie @prettygreenkitchen
Lauren is a bubbly blonde who was born, raised and is currently located in the beautiful
country of Scotland. Lauren is studying geography, which has left her with a extremely long
travel and adventure bucket list. She is also recovering from a long-term eating disorder and
is currently regaining her health. She attributes her progress massively to yoga, mindfulness
practice and finding joy in food and recipe creation.

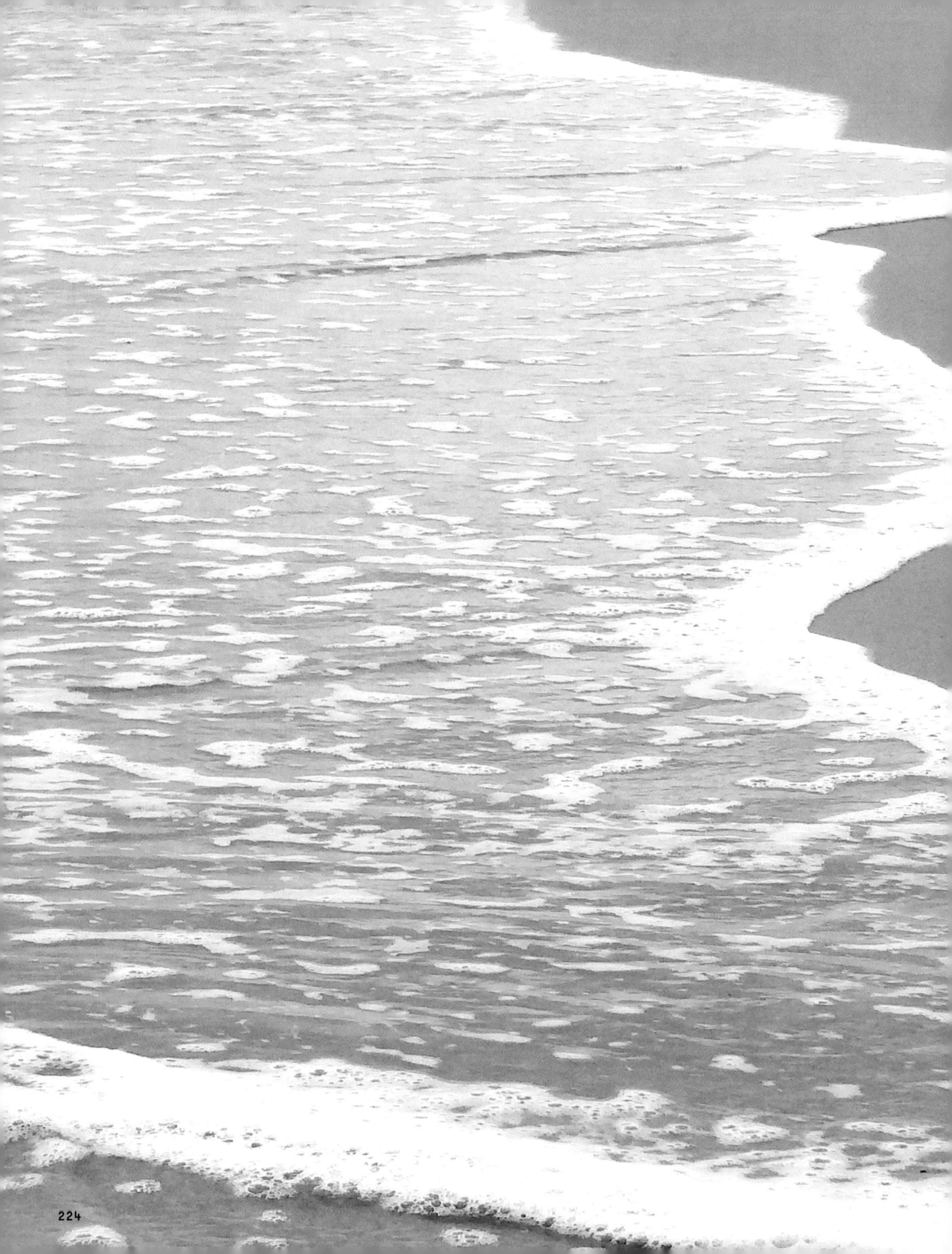

Small Bowls

SIDES - SNACKS

Small Bowls

Like every hero, a good meal needs a great sidekick - it's time to create some sensational sides! Let's oil that pan and prepare those breadcrumbs as it is time to create some sensational sides. We've got all kinds of fries and veggie nuggets ready to be drenched in delicious dipping sauces, plant-based mac and cheese and
everything in between.

When it comes to snacking on the go, a bit of preparation goes a long way. Perfect for you and a buddy, snack bars made with healthy granola, dried fruit and nuts make for a mouthful of goodness. Having a good repertoire of go-to snacks and sides is essential for maintaining a healthy diet and keeping your good spirits flourishing – and making sure you're not opting for something unhealthy when hunger strikes!

Once you've mastered your favourites, there are no limits to the combinations of ingredients you may want to try.

Go on, embrace your creative side. We think there's brilliance waiting to be discovered.

Veggie Nuggets with Sweet Chilli Dipping Sauce

These on-the-go healthy snacks are packed with fresh vegetables. Baked until crispy golden on the outside, they stay soft and moist on the inside. They're served here with a sticky, sweet and spicy dipping sauce, which is full of freshness.

MAKES 12+ NUGGETS

INGREDIENTS

Nuggets
- Coconut oil, for greasing
- 1 broccoli, coarsely chopped
- 1/2 cauliflower, coarsely chopped
- 2 carrots, coarsely chopped
- 2 cloves garlic, coarsely chopped
- 1 sweet red chilli, coarsely chopped
- 1 cup plain flour
- 3/4 cup polenta, plus extra for coating

Dipping Sauce
- 1/4 cup coconut sugar
- 1/4 cup coconut vinegar
- 1/2 cup water
- 2 long red chillies, finely sliced
- 1 clove garlic, minced
- 1/4 cup fresh coriander, chopped

METHOD

Nuggets
1. Pre-heat the oven to 180°C and line a baking tray with baking paper and grease with coconut oil.
2. In a high-speed blender, tip in all the vegetables, garlic and chilli. Blend until you have achieved a crumb-like texture.
3. Pour in a large bowl and squeeze out excess moisture, then stir through the flour and polenta until the mixture is sticky. The mixture needs to be able to be rolled into a ball and not fall apart – add flour if the mixture is not sticky enough.
4. Pour the extra polenta into a separate Coconut Bowl – you'll use this to crumb your nuggets.
5. Roll the nugget mixture into little balls, then flatten between your hands. Roll in the polenta to coat and place on the baking tray. Repeat.
6. Place nuggets in the oven to bake for 30 minutes, but keep an eye on them.

Dipping Sauce
7. Add the sugar, vinegar and water to a small saucepan and bring to the boil over a high heat. Simmer until the mixture has reduced by half.
8. Stir through the sliced chilli, garlic and coriander.
9. Serve the nuggets in your Coconut Bowls with a side of sauce.

Kadence Edmonds @featherandcrumb
Kadence lives on the Sunshine Coast, Queensland. Until recently, she worked in the food industry, where she gained a lot of knowledge on health food trends. Kadence loves food, and Feather and Crumb was born from that love. What started as an after-work hobby grew into a passion for turning basic foods into raw, rainbow, vegan delights.

Crispy Potato Chips with Guacamole

The classic potato wedge: irresistible to all. Baked with herbs and pepper and smothered in guacamole, this delicious snack is designed to share, but we won't judge if you just can't help yourself from finishing them all.

MAKES 4 BOWLS

INGREDIENTS

- 1.5kg potatoes, washed (or peeled) and quartered
- 2 tablespoons olive oil
- 1 tablespoon dried oregano
- 1 teaspoon pepper
- 1 avocado
- Juice of 1/2 lemon
- 1/2 teaspoon garlic, minced
- Salt

METHOD

1. Place potatoes in a large bowl and add the oil, oregano and 1/2 teaspoon of the pepper. Mix everything well.
2. Place the potato wedges onto a baking tray lined with baking paper. Make sure that the wedges don't touch each other. Bake for approximately 35–45 minutes at 200°C.
3. For the guacamole, mash the avocado in a small bowl and squeeze over lemon juice. Stir through the remaining pepper and garlic. Season to taste.
4. Serve the potato wedges in your Coconut Bowls and smother with guacamole dip.

Xenia Rehm @healthyhandsomelife
Xenia is the German vegan blogger behind healthyhandsomelife.com and is completely dedicated to her healthy, plant-based lifestyle. She also incorporates exercise, meditation, art and yoga into her daily routine. Xenia's biggest goals are to find happiness and to truly love herself and her life. She believes we are all students of life and that we should support each other to live it to the fullest.

Lu's Granola Bars

These soft, baked and chewy granola bars are a great breakfast option on the go or as a healthy snack between meals. Naturally sweetened with dates, these guilt-free bars will satisfy your cravings any time of the day.

MAKES 12+ BARS

INGREDIENTS

- 4 tablespoons chia seeds
- 400ml water
- 18 dates, pitted
- 3 tablespoons coconut oil, plus extra for greasing
- 2 cups oats
- 1/3 cup hemp seeds
- 1 1/2 cups pumpkin seeds
- 1 1/2 cups sunflower seeds
- 1/2 cup goji berries
- 1 tablespoon cinnamon
- 1 teaspoon vanilla

METHOD

1. Pre-heat oven to 190°C. Line a baking tray with baking paper and grease with coconut oil so the bars are easy to remove later.
2. In a small bowl, combine chia seeds with 150ml of the water. Leave to rest.
3. In a saucepan, heat dates and coconut oil over a low heat for 10–15 minutes.
4. Put dates in a high-speed blender with remaining water and blend until you get a smooth texture.
5. In a large bowl, mix together the oats, seeds, soaked chia seeds, goji berries, cinnamon and vanilla.
6. Stir through the date paste until well combined.
7. Spoon mixture onto the prepared tray and bake in the oven for approximately 30 minutes, until golden around the edges.
8. Leave to cool for about 15–20 minutes before cutting into bars.

Luisa Marsmann @luisamars
Luisa is a design student from Germany, however her heart yearns for a future at the beach, picking tropical fruit out of her window to make her morning smoothie bowls. Until then, she plans to travel around the world with her beloved camera around her neck, recording and soaking in all the natural beauty the world has to offer.

Popcorn Tofu

This simple recipe is a staple in my home because it is easy to make with ingredients that are always on hand. Popcorn tofu is also super fun to eat. It can be enjoyed as finger food on movie nights (just like popcorn), or served on a bed of rice with some veggies.

MAKES 2 BOWLS

INGREDIENTS

- 400g block extra firm tofu, drained and cut into small cubes
- 1 tablespoon olive oil
- 1/4 teaspoon garlic powder
- 1/4 teaspoon salt
- 1/4 teaspoon pepper
- 1/4 teaspoon red pepper flakes
- Sriracha sauce, to serve

METHOD

1. Pre-heat oven to 200°C.
2. On a non-stick baking tray, toss the tofu cubes with oil, garlic powder, salt, pepper and red pepper flakes until evenly coated. Spread tofu cubes across the pan, giving each cube space to breathe.
3. Bake for 20 minutes, flip or toss the tofu, and continue baking for another 10–20 minutes, depending on desired crispiness.
4. Serve tofu with sriracha on the side or drizzled on top.

Michelle Cehn @michellecehn @vegan @worldofvegan
Michelle is a photographer, filmmaker and YouTube personality on a mission to make plant-based living enticing and accessible to all. She is the founder of worldofvegan.com, co-author of *The Friendly Vegan Cookbook*, co-creator of The Dairy Detox and plantbasedmealplan.com. Michelle has reached millions through her creative, relatable and engaging videos, which you can find at youtube.com/worldofvegan.

Edamame Hummus & Oven Fries

Wow your friends and family with super tasty edamame hummus and oven fries! Both recipes are easy to prepare and make a comforting snack, while also being healthy and full of protein.

MAKES 2–4 BOWLS

INGREDIENTS

Fries

- 4 medium potatoes, washed and cut into 1cm-thick matchsticks
- 2–3 tablespoons extra virgin olive oil
- 1–2 teaspoons Himalayan salt

Edamame Hummus

- 1 cup chickpeas, drained
- 1 cup edamame, cooked and shelled, plus 1/4 cup to garnish
- 1/3 cup tahini
- 1/4 cup olive oil, plus extra to garnish
- 2 cloves garlic, peeled
- 1 tablespoon ground cumin
- Juice of 1 large lemon
- 1 teaspoon pink Himalayan salt
- 1 teaspoon ground pepper
- 1 tablespoon pine nuts, to garnish

METHOD

Fries

1. Pre-heat oven to 230°C and line an baking tray with baking paper.
2. Place potatoes into a bowl and cover with water. Allow to sit for at least 30 minutes to remove starch. Rinse and dry potatoes using paper towels.
3. Place potatoes, olive oil and salt into a large bowl. Mix well until potato is coated.
4. Transfer to baking tray and spread potatoes out to ensure there aren't any overlapping.
5. Bake for around 30–35 minutes, turning halfway through.

Edamame Hummus

6. While the fries are baking, prepare the hummus by adding chickpeas, edamame, tahini, olive oil, garlic, cumin and lemon juice to a high-speed blender. Blend until hummus is smooth and creamy. Taste and adjust seasoning as needed.
7. Transfer edamame hummus to your Coconut Bowls and drizzle with olive oil and pine nuts. Scatter extra edamame over the oven fries and hummus before serving.

Rachel Steenland @rachels.fit.kitchen
Rachel loves to cook, travel, take photos and share them with the world. After years flipping back and forth between traditional and vegetarian diets, she decided to trial a plant-based diet in 2015. It made her feel so good that she now lives a primarily plant-based lifestyle. After growing up on the sunny beaches of Australia's Sunshine and Gold Coasts, Rachel and her husband now live in the burbs of Boston.

Choc Chip Peanut Butter Clif-Style Bars

These are a healthy, homemade version of the popular Clif bars. They are crunchy for the first few hours after baking them, but then they become chewy. Dip into more peanut butter for a flavour party in your mouth.

MAKES 8 BARS

INGREDIENTS

- 1/2 cup dates, pitted and soaked
- 1/4 cup peanut butter
- 2 tablespoons of pure maple syrup
- 1/4 cup almond milk
- 1 cup rolled oats
- 1 cup rice bubbles
- 2 tablespoons of ground flaxseed
- 1/4 cup vegan vanilla protein powder
- 1/3 cup vegan dark chocolate chunks
- Coconut oil, for kneading

METHOD

1. Pre-heat oven to 160°C and line a baking tray with baking paper.
2. In a high-speed blender, blitz together the dates, peanut butter, maple syrup and almond milk until a creamy mixture forms.
3. In a large bowl, combine the oats, rice bubbles, flaxseed, protein powder and chocolate chunks and mix well.
4. Lightly coat your palms with coconut oil. Add the wet mixture to the dry and knead together until a dough forms.
5. Spread the dough into a large rectangle on the lined baking tray. Cut into smaller bars with a knife.
6. Bake for 15–20 minutes until golden and crispy.
7. Remove from the oven and allow to cool before serving.

Tip: Store in an airtight container at room temperature for up to 5 days.

Michelle Chen @run2food
Michelle is a future dentist with a passion for food. She loves sharing healthy, simple and delicious vegan recipes to inspire people to make a change for the better. Michelle is also a huge supporter of local eateries that support veganism. Michelle's goal is to show you how delicious vegan food is and how easy it can be to live a vegan lifestyle.

Sweet Potato Mac & Cheese

*This is an incredibly delicious vegan take on the classic mac and cheese!
It is super easy and quick to cook, and you'll probably have most of the
ingredients readily available at home.*

MAKES 2 BOWLS

INGREDIENTS

- 200g macaroni
- 20g spelt flour
- 1–2 tablespoons olive oil
- 1/2 cup sweet potato, cooked and mashed
- 1 cup dairy-free milk
- 1 clove garlic, minced
- 1–2 teaspoons mustard
- 1 teaspoon soy sauce
- Squeeze of lemon juice

METHOD

1. Bring a large pot of water to a boil. Cook the macaroni according to the package directions, then drain and rinse with cold water.
2. Mix the flour with the olive oil in a saucepan over medium heat – cook for 3 minutes.
3. Whisk in the mashed sweet potato, dairy-free milk, garlic, mustard, soy sauce and lemon juice. Add salt and pepper to taste.
4. As the mixture starts to bubble, reduce the heat and cook until thick.
5. Spoon the pasta into your Coconut Bowls, pour over the sauce and serve.

Yolanda Dawson @yolcsita_eats
Yolanda was born and raised in Hungary and is now living and studying in Berlin.
She discovered her passion for cooking and baking in her early teens, and she loves
cooking and eating healthy, delicious, plant-based food. Her dream is to become
a professional food photographer.

Veggie Fried Rice

Fried rice is such a versatile dish, as you can add as many ingredients as you like. This veggie fried rice can be enjoyed as a meal or a delicious side to the main event.

MAKES 2 BOWLS

INGREDIENTS

- 1 cup brown rice
- 2 tablespoons oil (of your choice)
- 1 medium carrot, diced
- 1 handful snow peas, diced
- 1 handful red capsicum, chopped
- 1 handful corn kernels
- 1 handful shiitake mushrooms
- 3 tablespoons soy sauce or tamari
- 1 handful spring onion, finely chopped
- Salt and pepper

METHOD

1. Cook brown rice over medium heat, following packet directions. Set aside to cool.
2. Heat wok or frying pan over medium heat. Add half the oil and swirl to coat.
3. Add all the vegetables to the frying pan and season with salt and pepper. Stir fry for 2 minutes, then add rest of oil.
4. Add the cooked rice to the vegetables and stir fry until rice is heated through and vegetables are cooked through. Add soy sauce or tamari and spring onion. Season with pepper.
5. Serve in your Coconut Bowls.

Grace Chung @breakinspiration

Born and raised in Mauritius, Grace has always been passionate about food. She moved to Melbourne to study hospitality management and was lucky enough to learn more about nutrition and wellness, and how to live healthy lifestyle. She began Breakinspiration with the goal of starting each day with a healthy, delicious and nutritious meal, and to inspire people to live a healthy, positive and, most importantly, happy life.

Potachos (Potato Nachos)

Crispy potatoes replace traditional corn chips in this recipe for plant-based nachos, but it is the salsa that is the real hero. Watch out: this recipe could very easily become your go-to snack!

MAKES 2 BOWLS

INGREDIENTS

- 4 medium potatoes, thinly sliced
- 1 tablespoon nutritional yeast
- 1 teaspoon garlic powder
- 1 teaspoon sweet paprika
- 1 teaspoon smoked paprika
- 100g cherry tomatoes, quartered
- 1/2 red onion, finely diced
- 1/2 jalapeno, thinly sliced
- Juice of 1/2 lemon
- 2 handfuls fresh coriander
- 3 tablespoons sweetcorn
- 1/2 avocado, diced
- 400g black beans (optional)

METHOD

1. Pre-heat the oven to 200°C.
2. In a small bowl, mix together the yeast, garlic and paprika. Place potato slices in a large bowl and sprinkle over seasoning and mix so each piece is perfectly coated.
3. Next, place the potatoes on a baking tray lined with baking paper and bake for 45 minutes.
4. In a medium-sized bowl, add the tomatoes, onion, jalapeno, lemon juice, a handful of coriander and combine to make a salsa.
5. Line the sides of your Coconut Bowls with the baked potato chips and top with sweetcorn, avocado, beans (if using) and salsa. Sprinkle over the remaining coriander and dig in.

Tereza Šlancarova @terezas_diary

Tereza is a life enthusiast based in the heart of Europe, the Czech Republic. She found her passion for healthy living about three years ago after struggling with body image issues. Tereza began her blog terezasdiary.com to try and help other girls not to make the same mistakes, and to encourage them to love the beauty we all have inside. Tereza also loves being active – she is a half-marathon competitor and certified yoga instructor.

Baked Zucchini Fries with Spicy Avocado Aioli

These zucchini fries are delicious. A crowd-pleasing appetiser, no matter the occasion, or an easy and tasty snack at any time of the day!

MAKES 2 SNACK BOWLS

INGREDIENTS

Fries

- 2 medium zucchini, sliced into fries (about 25mm wide)
- 1/2 cup almond milk
- 1/4 cup flour
- 1/4 teaspoon salt
- 1/4 teaspoon paprika
- 1/4 teaspoon garlic powder
- 1 cup breadcrumbs

Spicy Avocado Aioli

- 1 avocado, pitted and diced
- 1/2 jalapeno, chopped, plus extra slices to garnish
- 1/2 tablespoon lemon juice
- 1 teaspoon minced garlic
- 1/4 cup vegan mayo
- Pinch of salt and pepper

METHOD

Fries

1. Pre-heat oven to 220°C. Line a baking tray with baking paper and set aside.
2. Set up an assembly line with the milk in one bowl, flour and spices in another, and breadcrumbs in a third bowl.
3. Dip each zucchini fry in flour, then milk, then the breadcrumbs. Place them on the baking tray and continue until all are coated.
4. Bake for 18 minutes then grill for 2 minutes or until desired crispiness is achieved.

Spicy Avocado Aioli

5. Add all ingredients to a blender and blend until smooth. You may need to stop and scrape down the walls of the blender as needed.

To Serve

6. Line your Coconut Bowl with zucchini fries and serve with a good dollop of avocado aioli. Sprinkle with jalapeño slices.

Chad Montano @briewilly
Chad is a Californian native living in San Diego. He is a food photographer and food stylist with a deep passion for nutrition, health and fitness. Chad wants to inspire others to live a healthy lifestyle through proper nutrition and exercise. His mission in life is to not only survive but to thrive through passion, laughter and love.

Eat the Rainbow Fruit Salad

There's nothing better than a bowl of fresh, vibrant fruit. Whether this is your wake-up call or a lovely afternoon snack, you can never go wrong with a bowl of beautiful, nutrient-dense rainbow goodness. Keep it simple with whatever fruit you have on hand.

MAKES 2 BOWLS

INGREDIENTS

- 1 ripe banana
- 1 cup blueberries
- 2 cups papaya
- 1 plum
- 1 cup strawberries
- 1 tablespoon hemp seeds

METHOD

1. Simply chop the fruit as desired, place it in your Coconut Bowls and sprinkle with hemp seeds.

Ashley Hampton @rawincollege
Ashley is a passionate millennial determined to spread the positivity and power of a vegan lifestyle. As an activist, she strives to increase awareness and inspire others to go vegan through daily posts and creative content published on her social media and blog.

Eggplant & Pomegranate Boats

This simple snack will only take 30 minutes to prepare before you can devour it. It is mouthwatering and simple, with fresh vibrant flavours. This is a pre-dinner favourite that will get heads turning and mouths talking.

MAKES 2 BOATS

INGREDIENTS

- 1 eggplant, halved
- Dash of olive oil
- 1 pomegranate
- 2 tablespoons tahini
- 2 tablespoons lemon juice
- 2 tablespoons water
- 1 clove garlic, crushed
- Pinch of salt
- Fresh mint, to garnish

METHOD

1. Pre-heat oven to 200°C.
2. Using a knife, score eggplant flesh in a diamond pattern.
3. Brush the eggplant with olive oil and place in the oven for 30 minutes.
4. While the eggplant bakes, de-seed the pomegranate. The easy way is to cut it in half and then hold it in your hand while whacking the back with a spoon. All the seeds will fall out.
5. For the dressing, mix the tahini, lemon juice, water, garlic and salt together until well combined.
6. Take the eggplant out of the oven, drizzle with the dressing, cover in pomegranate seeds and top with some fresh mint.

Simon & Jaime Hall @messy.veggies
Jaime and Simon are the Australian vegan bloggers behind Messy Veggies. Initially a place to record their favourite recipes, Messy Veggies is now a blog and magazine that shows just how easy it is to live a plant-based life. After the recent diagnosis and removal of a brain tumour, Jaime still faces challenges in her everyday life. She has taken this opportunity to write about her experience and to talk about the taboo topic of cancer.

Plant-Based Mac & Cheese

This comforting and familiar dish is sure to bring back plenty of memories.
Pair your favourite macaroni with this rich creamy sauce, featuring a hint
of spice. Get creative and add cauliflower or broccoli florets.

MAKES 6 BOWLS

INGREDIENTS

- 2 cups potatoes,
  peeled and chopped
- 1/2 cup carrots,
  peeled and chopped
- 2/3 cup onion, chopped
- 1 clove garlic, chopped
- 2 cups water
- 1 cup raw cashews,
  soaked overnight
- 2/3 cup vegan butter
  or margarine
- 1 teaspoon salt
- 1 teaspoon turmeric
- 2 teaspoons Dijon mustard
- 2 tablespoons lemon juice
- 1/2 teaspoon pepper
- 1/2 teaspoon paprika
- 500g pasta of your choice

METHOD

1. In a large pot, add vegetables and water and bring to a boil. Reduce heat and simmer for 15 minutes.
2. While the vegetables are cooking, put cashews, butter, salt, turmeric, mustard, lemon juice, pepper and paprika in a high-speed blender.
3. When the vegetables are ready, pour the entire contents of the pot (water included) into the blender.
4. Blend for 2 minutes, until the mixture is completely smooth, with no chunks. You want the mixture as creamy as possible.
5. Cook your pasta according to the instructions on the package (al dente is best) and drain.
6. Using about 1/2 cup of sauce per 100g of pasta, pour the sauce over the drained pasta and mix with a large spoon.
7. Serve in your Coconut Bowls.

Victoria & Christopher Bill @ehvegan
Victoria and Christopher are a vegan couple from Montreal, Canada. They love to share their passion for vegan cooking and delicious recipes for others to enjoy. Victoria and Christopher also love travelling and exploring all the amazing plant-based food the world has to offer.

Basics

VEGAN PESTO - ALMOND MILK - GUACAMOLE - SATAY SAUCE

Five-Minute Vegan Pesto

MAKES 1 CUP BY TALINE GABRIELIAN

INGREDIENTS

- 3/4 cup (95g) walnuts
- 2 cloves garlic
- 2 bunches basil leaves
- 1/2 teaspoon sea salt (or to taste)
- 1/4 teaspoon pepper
- Juice of 1 lemon
- 1 cup light olive oil

METHOD

1. Put walnuts in a high-speed blender and pulse until large crumbs form.
2. Add garlic, basil, salt, pepper and lemon juice. Pulse.
3. Add olive oil and process until smooth.

Almond Milk

MAKES 1L BY LONI JANE

INGREDIENTS

- 1 cup almonds
- 1/2 teaspoon vanilla extract (or another pure extract of choice)
- 1 Medjool date, pitted (optional)

METHOD

1. Place your almonds in a glass jar and top with water. Let the almonds soak for 12–24 hours.
2. After soaking the almonds, rinse well with fresh water then place in a high-speed blender with 1 litre fresh drinking water, plus vanilla and the pitted date to sweeten, if using.
3. Blend on high for 4 minutes.
4. Hang a nut milk bag or cheesecloth over a bowl. Pour the almond mixture into the bag or cloth and strain, squeezing all the liquid from the pulp.
5. Using a funnel or pouring jug, pour the milk into a glass bottle and seal tightly with a close-fitting lid.
6. Store in the fridge for up to 5 days.

Guacamole

MAKES 1 CUP   BY SIRI HARSEM

INGREDIENTS

- 1 large avocado
- 2 cloves garlic, crushed
- 2 tablespoons coriander leaves, finely chopped
- Juice of 1/2 lime
- Salt and pepper

METHOD

1. In a large bowl, mash the avocado with a fork. Add garlic, coriander and lime juice.
2. Mix all the ingredients together and add salt and pepper to taste.

Satay Sauce

MAKES1/4CUP   BY TINA KHOURY

INGREDIENTS

- 1 bunch fresh coriander, stems and roots finely sliced
- 1 tablespoon date syrup (maple or rice syrup works too)
- 2 small cloves garlic
- 2cm piece of ginger
- Zest of 1 lime
- 4 tablespoons lime juice
- 1/4 cup smooth peanut butter
- 1–2 small red chillies (according to taste)
- Pinch of sea salt

METHOD

1. Combine all the ingredients in a high-speed blender and blend until you reach a sauce-like consistency. If needed, add a tablespoon of water at a time, while blending, to thin out the mixture.
2. Store in the fridge for up to 5 days.

Index

"I was so incredibly excited to get my paws on these beautiful bowls! Although the Instagram page is amazing, the bowls are even more beautiful in person. The durability, shape and colours are so unique, and I'm so happy to support such a eco-conscious company. I can't wait to give the other bowls and spoons as thoughtful gifts to my friends and family!"

— TASHA B

About Coconut Bowls

Coconut Bowls is an Australian brand that develops eco-friendly natural products from waste materials. We source discarded coconut shells from coconut farms and wooden offcuts from furniture makers in Vietnam and Indonesia, before engaging local craftspeople to turn this waste into upcycled products that are perfect for your kitchen.

People are at the heart of what we do. All our Coconut Bowls, bamboo straws, wooden spoons, forks and chopsticks are handcrafted by local people. No part of our production process is outsourced to manufacturing machinery. Made by nature and crafted by hand, we pride ourselves on the quality of our products, and by making everything with our hands, we ensure long lasting durable natural products.

Environmental sustainability is very important to us, and our mission is to continue to develop innovative products from natural materials, preserving the raw beauty of each material.

We strive to raise awareness about sustainability through our brand and to inspire you to be eco-conscious with your decisions. We encourage you to be mindful of your waste, and to avoid using materials that cannot be recycled at every opportunity.

What we put in our bowls has a big impact on the environment, and fortunately eating healthier often means eating more sustainably. When we prioritise plants, we are benefiting both our body and the planet.

Through our community, we aim to educate you on the benefits of eating more plants, motivate you to try vegan recipes and to help you eat more mindfully. May we all prepare beautiful, wholesome food with love and be grateful for making conscious food choices that are kinder on the world.

Join our community at coconutbowls.com or on social media @coconutbowls.

Acknowledgments

To Jonette, Daniele, Katie and the entire Smudge Publishing team, I am
so grateful for all your guidance, support and patience with this project.
Your expertise and experience have helped make Vegan Bowls the most
beautiful cookbook that I could ever imagine. From our first meeting,
you gave me the confidence to push ahead and to not only create the
product that I had envisioned but to make it even better. I thank you so, so
much for everything. You have an amazing team and I could not wish for
a better publishing partner.